THE LEGAL
COMPANION

Vincent Powell

Introduction by Clive Anderson

A THINK BOOK FOR

ROBSON BOOKS

As formerly we suffered from crimes, so now we suffer from laws.

Cornelius Tacitus

THINK
A Think Book
for Robson Books

First published in Great Britain in 2005 by
Robson Books
The Chrysalis Building, Bramley Road, London W10 6SP

An imprint of **Chrysalis** Books Group plc

Text © Think Publishing 2005
Design and layout © Think Publishing 2005
The moral rights of the author have been asserted

Edited by Vincent Powell
Companion team: Tilly Boulter, James Collins, Rhiannon Guy, Emma Jones,
Jo Swinnerton, Lou Millward Tait, Malcolm Tait and Marcus Trower

Think Publishing
The Pall Mall Deposit
124-128 Barlby Road, London W10 6BL
www.thinkpublishing.co.uk

ISBN 1-86105-838-1

Printed in Italy

A jury consists of 12 persons chosen to decide who has the better lawyer.

Robert Lee Frost

A CASE FOR THANKS

This book would not have been possible without the determined research, inspired ideas, and dogged support of:

Alisa Hirschfeld, Alex Smith, Amshula Ghumman,
Brian Miller, Gabriel Powell, Jay Smith,
Lois Lee, Nicola Haynes, Selina Erhan, Solomon Powell,
Judy Darley, Felicity Egerton, Lois Lee,
Dave Pigeon, Nancy Waters

INTRODUCTION

Lawyers have never enjoyed a great reputation.

'Let's kill all the lawyers' (Dick, *Henry VI Part 2*, Shakespeare)

'What do you call 15 lawyers at the bottom of the Hudson River?' – 'A start'. (New York joke)

Devious, untrustworthy individuals prepared to bend the truth, twist the language and distort the facts for their own ends.

And they have their bad side as well.

The law itself is scarcely better regarded – according to Dickens' Mr Bumble, the law is a ass a idiot.

According to Robert Frost, a jury consists of 12 persons chosen to decide who has the better lawyer.

Perhaps this collection of legal related facts and *obiter dicta* will restore the reputation of the law and lawyers, though I doubt it. And I speak as a graduate, of what is here declared to be the best law school in the country.

But lawyers and non-lawyers alike will find many intriguing bits of information, some of it more useful than others in this fascinating little book. The design of a judge's wig, the pattern of the tartan of the Province of Ontario, the laws of Salon of Athens are all discussed, as well as some famous lawyers of fact and fiction.

Ignorance of the law is famously no excuse. But some considerable knowledge of the law is here a perfect excuse for an entertaining trip around some dusty corners of the legal world.

If you have the misfortune to get mixed up in the law, you may find this a perfect volume to browse through while you wait for your case to be reached. If you have never been mixed up in the law, it will give you some idea of what you are missing.

Clive Anderson

TOP NOTCH

The judge's wig of today has a notch on the top. This serves as a reminder of the white coif, which was the judge's original headdress as determined by the Judges' Rules of 1635. A black skullcap was worn over the white coif and another black cap on top. As the use of wigs rose in popularity, this style of headdress was superceded about 50 years after the 1635 rules were laid down, but the coif remains symbolically on a judge's head to this day.

CRIMINAL MISTAKES

A man charged with drug possession in Pontiac, Michigan claimed he'd been searched illegally. The police said they saw a bulge in his pocket that could have been a gun. As he was wearing the same jacket in court, still with its bulge, he was able to prove the bulge wasn't a gun – unfortunately for him it was a bag of cocaine.

In Oklahoma City a man who was accused of armed robbery made the mistake in court of losing his temper when he was identified by the store manager, saying that he should have blown her head off. Needless to say, he was found guilty.

A peeping Tom in Virginia left lip prints on a window. When he returned a few days later he was arrested and a positive lip match sent him to prison.

A man who robbed a supermarket in Long Beach was later arrested at home. He'd filled out a credit application form earlier at the same supermarket and was recognised.

QUOTE UNQUOTE

Laws are like sausages. It's better not to see them being made.
Otto von Bismarck, first Chancellor of the German Empire

NARCS AND NOSES

The word 'narc', meaning an officer of the law specialising in drugs cases, has an obvious derivation from 'narcotic'. However, the word was also used to refer to a police informant or indeed a policeman in Britain in the 1890s. It derives from the Romany word 'naak' meaning 'nose' – in other words, an informer or an officer is someone who sticks their nose into other people's business. There was an equivalent in Cockney rhyming slang which was 'norze', which itself stood for 'Noah's Ark'. The contemporary American and older British terms are unlikely to be related.

10 *Percentage that domestic vehicle thefts were down in 2003–04 from 2002–03 in England and Wales, according to the British Crime Survey*

LITERATURE AND THE LAW

I don't hit the buzzer to change my story. I hit it because my story ain't getting told. I get an enlightenment about the 10 years it feels like I've been listening to this whole crowd of powerdime spinners, with their industry of carpet-fibre experts, and shrinks and all, who finish me off with their goddam blah, blah, blah. And you just know the State ain't flying any experts down for me. What I learned is you need that industry, big-time. Because, although you ain't allowed to say it, and I hope I ain't doing The Devil's Work by saying it myself – Reasonable Doubt just don't apply any more. Not in practice, don't try and tell me it does. Maybe if your cat bit the neighbour's hamster, like with Judge Judy or something. But once they ship in extra patrol cars, and build a zoo cage in court, forget it. You have to come up with simple, honest-to-goodness proof of innocence, that anybody can tell just by watching TV. Otherwise they hammer through nine centuries of technical evidence, like a millennium of back-to-back math classes, and it's up in there that they wipe out Reasonable Doubt.

DBC Pierre, *Vernon God Little*

LEGAL QUANDARIES

J, a barman, is in the habit of serving liquor to an off-duty policeman, K. K takes his armband off when he is off-duty. One day J serves K, in the usual way. But K is actually on duty. Is J guilty of serving liquor to an on-duty officer?
Answer on page 153

IGNORANCE OF THE LAW IS NO DEFENCE

Whether you're a lawmaker, citizen or criminal, there's always a law out there waiting to be broken.

For example, it is illegal for a British MP to turn up for work in a suit of armour. An easy mistake to make in the morning when you're still half-asleep as you blunder around for something to wear.

In Australia, you can't wander the streets wearing felt shoes, black clothes and black shoe polish on your face in case you are mistaken for a criminal.

Criminals must also be aware of the etiquette of crime. In Seattle, a person intending to commit a crime is obliged, upon entering the city limits, to inform the Chief of Police of their plans. Similarly, in Texas criminals must give oral or written notice to a potential victim explaining the nature of the crime to be committed. It's only polite, really.

Cuthbert was astonished. Five crimes, five identity parades, five times successfully picked out. Perhaps, he mused, he should wear less conspicuous trousers.

THE REAL DEVIL'S ADVOCATE

French lawyer Jacques Verges has earned himself the name 'The Devil's Advocate' because of the clients he represents. During World War II, Verges was a member of the French resistance and fought against the Nazis. Then, as a young man, he built up a reputation as a tenacious lawyer who defended Algerians tortured by the French military. The turning point in his career, when he went from being a champion of the left to a vilified advocate in the eyes of many, was his decision in 1983 to defend Klaus Barbie, the Nazi head of the Gestapo. Verges says his instincts called for him to step in because Barbie was on course for a lynching. Although Verges' clients are usually found guilty, he is an expert at turning high profile cases around and pointing the finger at accusers. Other clients he has represented include: Khieu Samphan, Pol Pot's accomplice in the genocide of Cambodians; the terrorist Carlos the Jackal; and Slobodan Milosevic, former leader of Serbia. But arguably his most famous client has been one of his most recent: none other than Saddam Hussein, the former dictator of Iraq.

In 1895, the three trials involving Oscar Wilde at the Old Bailey in London set the literary world and the chattering classes of England alight. The events that saw Wilde take the stand began in 1891 when he met Lord Alfred Douglas, or 'Bosie' as Wilde affectionately called him. Bosie was a talented, aspiring 22-year-old poet to Wilde's 38-year-old literary heavyweight. The two became fast friends; Bosie was impressed by Wilde's status and attentions, and Wilde by Bosie's poems – and his beauty.

The closeness of the friendship was viewed unkindly by Bosie's father, John Douglas, the Marquess of Queensberry, an irascible Scot with a reputation for being difficult. Douglas' interests tended more toward boxing than literature – he was renowned for developing the rules of amateur boxing known as the Queensberry rules. Despite being initially charmed over lunch by Wilde, Douglas became convinced that his son's new friend was a homosexual and began going to great lengths to dissuade Bosie from fraternising with Wilde.

One day Douglas and a boxer turned up at Wilde's London flat and there was an argument. Wilde said, 'I do not know what the Queensberry rules are, but the Oscar Wilde rule is to shoot on sight.' Douglas left, but began to spread damaging rumours of Wilde's homosexuality. Wilde, despite being advised against it by friends such as George Bernard Shaw, decided to take legal action against him.

In March 1895 Douglas was arrested and charged with libel. Wilde employed the services of Edward Clarke, a high-flying London barrister. At the trial, Clarke gave a powerful performance, but cracks began to appear under the cross-examination of Edward Carson, an old Trinity College rival. Wilde, ever witty and suave, replied to a question as to whether he kissed a particular boy: 'Oh, dear no! He was a particularly plain boy.' Following Carson's announcement that he intended to call as witnesses boys with whom Wilde had been sexually associated, Wilde and Clarke withdrew the libel action.

However, on the strength of the witness statements prepared on Douglas' behalf, the police arrested Wilde. The second trial began in April 1895, this time with Wilde as the defendant. A number of young men testified about their relations with Wilde. After three hours of deliberation, the jury could not reach a verdict and Wilde was released on bail. Three weeks later the third trial began. Many of the same young men gave testimony again and this time England's most successful prosecutor, Frank Lockwood, secured a conviction. Wilde served two years in prison, where he continued to write (works included *De Profundis* and *The Ballad of Reading Gaol*). He was released in 1897 and died in Paris in 1900 at the age of 46.

There are laws and regulations made on a huge number of subjects of greater or lesser importance. Sometimes it is difficult to understand what prompts new laws. Here, in no particular order, is a brief history of a few of the more unusual ones and a few thoughts on what might have inspired them.

Chrysanthemum (Temporary Prohibition on Landing) (Great Britain) Order 1980 – lawmakers had read *The Day of the Triffids* and when they saw the boat approaching, they knew they had to act quickly.

Cider and Perry Regulations 1989 – Perry was notorious for causing trouble after a few pints.

Wild Birds (Sundays) Order 1955 – the Day of Rest should apply to all species.

Cattle Passports Order 1996 – Following rumours of foot-and-mouth disease, the Home Office was flooded with applications from cattle desperate to leave Britain.

Mines (Manner of Search for Smoking Materials) Order 1956 – the way in which miners located packets of B&H underwent standardisation.

Rabies (Importation of Dogs, Cats and Other Mammals) (Amendment) Order 1986 – after a show of hands, it was decided that importing rabid animals wasn't such a good idea.

Arsenic in Food Regulations 1959 – proper labelling was needed to make clear the likelihood of death following ingestion of arsenic-laden foods.

Wild Birds (Sunday in Anglesey) Order 1963 – wild birds in Anglesey initially resisted the 1955 regulations.

Radioactive Substances (Schools, etc) Exemption Order 1963 – it was roundly concluded that schools weren't the best place to store uranium.

Radioactive Substances (Tokens for Vending Machines) Exemption Order 1968 – the wisdom of selling plutonium alongside the crisps had come into question.

Scotch Whiskey Order 1990 – it had been a long day in Parliament, so MPs clubbed together to buy a bottle of spirits from the offie.

QUOTE UNQUOTE

My guiding principle is this: guilt is never to be doubted.
Franz Kafka, Czech writer

The magistrate lets oot a sharp exhalation. It isnae a brilliant job the cunt's goat, whin ye think aboot it. It must git pretty tiresome dealin wi radges aw day. Still, ah bet the poppy's fuckin good, n naebody's asking the cunt tae dae it. He should try tae be a wee bit mair professional, a bit mair pragmatic, rather than showin his annoyance so much.

Mr Renton, you did not intend to sell the books?

Naw. Eh, no, your honour. They were for reading.

So you read Kierkegaard. Tell us about him, Mr Renton, the patronising cunt sais.

I'm interested in his concepts of subjectivity and truth, and particularly his ideas concerning choice; the notion that genuine choice is made out of doubt and uncertainty, and without recourse to the experience or advice of others. It could be argued, with some justification, that it's primarily a bourgeois, existential philosophy and would therefore seek to undermine collective societal wisdom. However, it's also a liberating philosophy, because when such societal wisdom is negated, the basis for social control over the individual becomes weakened and... but I'm rabbiting a bit here. Ah cut myself short. They hate a smart cunt. It's easy to talk yourself into a bigger fine, or fuck sake, a higher sentence. Think deference Renton, think deference.

The magistrate snorts derisively. As an educated man ah'm sure he kens far mair aboot the great philosophers than a pleb like me. Yiv goat tae huv fuckin brains tae be a fuckin judge. S no iviry cunt thit kin dae that fuckin joab.

Irvine Welsh, *Trainspotting*

RELIGION AND THE LAW

Judaism

Jewish law is called 'Halakhah', which in Hebrew means 'The path one walks'. Judaism is a set of rules that covers all aspects of life, both secular and religious. It deals with a person's spirituality and relationship with God and with a person's relationship to other people. It governs every aspect of practical everyday life. Though based on the Torah, Jewish law is not exclusively sourced from this but also from traditions and takkanot, which are laws that come from rabbis. A takkanah can vary from place to place and can occasionally be changed. The Torah is made up of 613 mitzvot or commandments, though the word mitzvah may also refer more generally to any tradition or law under Halakhah. A gezeirah is a rule by a rabbi that clarifies a mitzvah, and it can sometimes be changed. The Torah is not a formal code of law but is a source of law and legislation.

MOST PROLIFIC SERIAL KILLERS

Ranked in order of number of victims

Who	Where	When	How many
1= Harold Shipman	Great Britain	1970s, 80s & 90s	300 approx
1= Pedro Alonso Lopez	Peru, Colombia and Ecuador	1970s	300 approx
3 Henry Lee Lucas and Ottis Toole	America	1960s & 70s	200 approx
4 Herman Mudgett	Chicago	1890s	200 approx
5 Pee Wee Gaskins	America	1960s	100 approx
6 Nikolai Dzhurmongaliev	Russia	1980s	100 approx
7 Delfina and Maria de Jesus Gonzales	Mexico	1950s & 60s	91
8 Bruno Ludke	Germany	1930s & 40s	81
9 Andrei Chikatilo	Russia	1980s & 90s	52 approx
10 Anatoly Onoprienko	Ukraine	1990s	52

DIPLOMATIC IMMUNITY

The thought of visiting a country and being in any way exempt from the normal process of taxation and law may be appealing, but it is something reserved for only a small number of VIPs: foreign diplomats. The origin of the immunity dates back to ancient times, when the Greeks would offer foreign envoys an immunity to domestic laws. The more recent version of this tradition was set out at the 1961 Vienna Convention on Diplomatic Relations. The policy cites how and why the immunity works, emphasising the promotion of friendliness between nations while pointing out such privileges and immunities are not to benefit individuals but are also to ensure the efficient performance of the functions of diplomatic missions representing states. The Foreign Office defines the immunity as 'fundamental', allowing diplomats to work in often very difficult situations abroad. Diplomatic immunity has been criticised in cases where diplomats have been suspected of committing serious offences. However, the Foreign Office has said that only 21 out of 20,000 diplomats have been accused of serious offences. It seems that the vast majority of diplomats obey the laws of their host nations despite their immunity.

16 *Number of federal officials, including two presidents, impeached by the House of Representatives since 1797*

With this ring...

Though there is some historical suggestion that the wedding ring is the symbol of the bonds that barbarian husbands used to secure brides to their home, it was first used as a symbol in ancient Egypt circa 2800 BC.

In Roman times a woman wore a gold wedding ring in public, slipping into something more comfortable, an iron ring, when at home. Some rings from this era had a small key attached, which reflected the law that a woman was in partnership with her husband and thus shared his wealth.

Engagement rings predated wedding rings. Their use, among Roman Catholics at least, was codified by Pope Nicholas I who declared in 860 AD that an engagement ring was required for couples planning to marry. Diamond engagement rings were brought into vogue in the late 1400s by wealthy Venetians. In England, Princess Mary (1516-58), who became known as Bloody Mary for her persecution of Protestantism, was given one on her betrothal to the dauphin of France at the tender age of two. By the 1600s, diamond engagement rings were very much in fashion for those who could afford one.

I JUST DON'T KNOW WHAT TO WEAR

We all recognise the judge as the person wearing a wig and robe, but their choice of dress is more complicated than you might think. Fortunately, however, there is now a document to help them decide what to wear, so they can concentrate on more important things. The following Consultation Paper on court dress was issued on behalf of the Lord Chief Justice and the Lord Chancellor in August 1992 to clear things up: 'When sitting in the Court of Appeal (Criminal Division), High Court judges, like other members of the Court of Appeal, wear a black silk gown and a short wig, as they do in Divisional Court. When dealing with criminal business at first instance in the winter, a High Court judge wears the scarlet robe of the ceremonial dress but without the scarlet cloth and fur mantle. When dealing with criminal business in the summer, the judge wears a similar scarlet robe, but with silk rather than fur facings. A Queen's Bench judge trying civil cases in winter wears a black robe faced with fur, a black scarf and girdle and a scarlet tippet; in summer, a violet robe faced with silk, with the black scarf and girdle and scarlet tippet. On red letter days (which include the Sovereign's birthday and certain saint's days) all judges wear the scarlet robe for the appropriate season.'

GIVE ME DEATH?

'Give me freedom or give me death!' was the line Mel Gibson made famous in his movie *Braveheart* about the Scottish leader William Wallace. Unfortunately, he was taken at his word. Wallace defeated the forces of Edward I of England at Stirling in 1297, but in 1298 he was routed at Falkirk, tried and sentenced to death. He was hanged, drawn and quartered, which gave the triumphant authorities a chance to make the most of his dead body. His head was impaled on London Bridge; his left arm was displayed in Berwick; his right arm in Newcastle; his left leg in Aberdeen; and his right leg in Perth.

QUOTE UNQUOTE

The lawgiver, of all beings, most owes the law allegiance. He of all men should behave as though the law compelled him. But it is the universal weakness of mankind that what we are given to administer we presently imagine we own.
HG Wells, novelist

SILENT WITNESS

According to the memoirs of Justice Gerald Sparrow, a barrister who worked as a judge in Thailand in the 1900s, a slander case was once decided by a witness who said nothing. The dispute arose between two traders named Swee Ho and Pu Lin. Pu Lin had made comments at a party which challenged Swee Hoo's manhood. The comments were to the effect that Swee Ho was unable to please his wife or, for that matter, any woman. In court Swee Ho called his wife as a witness and though she just stood at the witness stand and said nothing, his case was proven – for it was clear to everyone in court that she was pregnant.

COUGHLIN'S LAWS

Coughlin's Laws in the 1988 movie *Cocktail*, starring Tom Cruise, about bartending and finding yourself, were a series of learned reflections on life by Tom's mentor, Doug Coughlin. A few of the more highbrow observations and rules for life were:
'Anything else is always something better.'
'Beer is for breakfast.'
'Don't talk unless you can improve the silence.'
'Champagne. Perfume going in, sewage coming out.'
'Bury the dead, they stink up the joint.'

Agatha's lawyer agreed that she might indeed have a case for suing her plastic surgeon.

NOTORIOUS PRISONS

Spandau

Spandau prison was built specifically to house Nazi war criminals convicted during the Nuremberg Trials following World War II, of which there were only seven – Karl Doenitz, Walther Funk, Rudolph Hess, Konstantin von Neurath, Erich Raeder, Baldur von Schirach and Albert Speer. The prison was operated by America, Britain, France and the Soviet Union, one of only two four-power organisations during the Cold War (the other was the Berlin Air Safety Centre). The four powers took turns to control the prison, rotating on a monthly basis. Their four flags hung together, and they were also rotated, the left-most flag signifying who had control of the prison that month. During the last 21 years of its existence, Spandau's only prisoner was Hess. The prison was closed when he died in 1987. The site is now a car park, and the materials from which the prison was built were ground into powder and scattered onto the North Sea.

THE DOG-BITE LAW

In the US, dog-bite law has almost become a genre unto itself, with laws covering everything from the legal rights of a dog-bite victim to landlords' rights and liabilities, and from the rights of a dog attack rescuer to the right of children to surgery for disfigurement by dogs. Some serious penalties can apply. For example, in Wyoming a dog owner can receive up to 20 years in prison if a person is killed by a dog that has been mistreated. If you need advice on dog-bite law in the US, look no further than attorney Kenneth Phillips. *Time Magazine* called him 'California's leading dog-bite lawyer', and *Lawyers' Weekly* called him 'the dog-bite king'. He has appeared on numerous TV and radio shows across the US. As the leading authority, he is in demand because of the startling number of incidents involving dog bites – five million a year, with 800,000 victims requiring medical treatment. Hospital emergency rooms across the nation admit 1,000 dog bite victims every day and the economic loss is estimated at US$1 billion every year. Half the victims are children, and most of them are bitten in the face, usually by a dog owned by a neighbour or friend – or by their own dog.

Dog bites are on the rise in the US. A recent study showed that the number of incidents has risen by a third over the last 10 years. For claims arising from dog bites, the insurance industry paid out $250 million in 1995, $310 million in 2001, and $345 million in 2002.

The problem isn't confined to the US. In Australia there is a new Super Dog on the loose, the offspring of escaped bull mastiffs and rottweilers that have mated with the dingo, Australia's wild native dog (special canine contact lenses may be a solution). Injuries to people are escalating and sheep flocks in the outback have been devastated. The government is struggling to introduce laws to stem the problem.

Next time you curse when you stand in dog poo, remember that it could have been a lot worse.

LEGAL QUANDARIES

B was out drinking with T. T intended to drive home later, so was drinking tonic water. B did not want T to drive home but to spend the night with her, so she added vodka to his tonic water, knowing that he would not drive when she later told him she'd spiked his drinks. However, before B could tell T what she'd done, he drove away. He was charged with driving under the influence. Is B guilty of aiding and abetting T to commit the offence?
Answer on page 153

WITCH GUILT

Witchcraft has been around for centuries, and for most of that time it has been illegal. In medieval times, one method for discovering whether a woman was a witch was by 'swimming'. With her right big toe tied to her left thumb, and her left big toe tied to her right thumb, she was unceremoniously thrown into the nearest pond. If she floated she was guilty, as it meant that the devil was assisting her. If she sank, she was innocent – which was fine as long as she could be rescued in time to benefit from her acquittal. Another less unfair method of determining guilt was to weigh a woman against the church bible. If she was lighter, then she was a witch. One of history's most famous 'witches' was Joan of Arc, who was burned at the stake in 1431 at the age of 19, having been found guilty of witchcraft. French memories were short – two years before, she had been a heroine, leading an army against the English. But before we congratulate ourselves for leaving behind such barbaric behaviour, it is worth noting that a woman named Josefina Arista was burnt as a witch in Mexico as recently as 1956.

LITERATURE AND THE LAW

The present state of our knowledge of the history of our law may be likened to an unfinished building, whose foundations have been laid and whose frame and beams have been erected. The roof, the walls, the floors, the furnishings and decoration, are yet lacking. Its scope and internal plan, its architecture and its relation of parts, can be already plainly seen. But it cannot yet be inhabited; and many kinds of workmen must labour longer upon it.

**The Committee of the Association of
American Law Schools, 1907**

A LEGAL PINT

If you fancy sitting down somewhere for a quiet pint to contemplate some of the finer points of the law, here are a few pubs that may be conducive to thoughts of a legal nature.

Old Court House Inn – *St Aubin, Channel Islands*
Golden Rule – *Ambleside, Cumbria*
Highwayman – *Sourton, Devon*
Wig & Mitre – *Lincoln, Lincolnshire*
Double Locks – *Exeter*
Fox Goes Free – *Charlton*
Old Dungeon Ghyll – *Langdale, Cheshire*
Hanging Gate – *Langley, Cheshire*
Bitter End – *Cockermouth, Cumbria*

Masonic Lodges throughout the world have some autonomy over their own lodge rules and can vary them to suit themselves. However, one unbending feature of Masonic law is its strong stance on alcohol. For example, in North Carolina, their law states, 'Drunkenness is a serious Masonic offence.'

In the US there are three states – North Carolina, Georgia, and Arkansas – in which you cannot become a Mason if you run a liquor business.

In Texas, the Masonic law says, 'Thou Shalt Not... indulge in the intemperate use of intoxicating liquor, gambling or profane swearing.'

In West Virginia they state, 'Intemperance is unmasonic, and it is insisted that every Lodge strictly and diligently discipline any member... who shall... become intoxicated.' But it is not just the Mason who might be punished. In Alabama their law says 'any Mason who visits a lodge or participates in a Masonic procession or funeral while intoxicated is guilty of unmasonic conduct, and if his lodge does not prefer charges against him the "derelict" lodge is to be reported to the Grand Master or Grand Lodge.'

However, a Mason from Louisiana noted with some distress a lodge meeting where this general trend was not being observed: 'I have been to Scottish Rite Lodges in New Orleans where alcohol has been served, but this has been a few years back. It seems that our Grand Lodge does not have the power to rule on this.' It seems that Scottish traditions run deeper than Masonic ones...

LATIN TERMS REINVENTED

Latin terms are used often in the law, but how do we know what they mean? Here are a few that could easily be misunderstood, along with their real meanings ...

Latin term	Seems to mean	Actually means
Ab extra	Advert for a gym	From outside
Bona fide	Dog food	Good faith
Bona vacantia	No dog food	Goods without an owner
De die in diem	Coffins	Day to day
De futuro	A new Italian car	In the future
De integro	The sedan model	Regarding the whole
De lege lata	A strong coffee	What the law says
Doli incapax	Unable to sign on the dole	Unable to commit a crime
Jus	A refreshing drink	A legally recognised right
Orse	An annoying person	Otherwise

22 *Minimum legal length, in inches, for the commercial sale of Californian halibut*

Dr Van Helsing speaking to Mina Harker, as recorded in her Journal, about Count Dracula, driven from England; yet, like a tiger with a taste for human blood driven from a village in India, he plans to return:

This that we hunt from our village is a tiger, too, a man-eater, and he never cease to prowl. Nay, in himself he is not one to retire and stay afar. In his life, his living life, he go over the Turkey frontier and attack his enemy on his own ground; he be beaten back, but did he stay? No! He come again, and again, and again. Look at his persistence and endurance. With the child-brain that was to him he have long since conceive the idea of coming to a great city. What does he do? He find out the place of all the world most of promise for him. Then he deliberately set himself down to prepare for the task. He find in patience just how is his strength, and what are his powers. He study new tongues. He learn new social life; new environment of old ways, the politic, the law, the finance, the science, the habit of a new land and a new people who have come to be since he was. His glimpse that he have had, whet his appetite only and enkeen his desire. Nay, it help him to grow as to his brain; for it all prove to him how right he was at the first in his surmises. He have done this alone; all alone! from a ruin tomb in a forgotten land. What more may he not do when the greater world of thought is open to him? He that can smile at death, as we know him; who can flourish in the midst of diseases that kill off whole peoples. Oh! if such an one was to come from God, and not the Devil, what a force for good might he not be in this old world of ours!

Bram Stoker, *Dracula*

THE SERIOUS MATTER OF ASSAULT

As of 2004, the countries with the highest number of serious assaults per head of population were, in descending order:

1. Australia
2. Sweden
3. Swaziland
4. South Africa
5. Belgium
6. Namibia
7. Ghana
8. New Zealand
9. Botswana
10. Jamaica
11. United States
12. Argentina

Number of women among the 135 judges who sit in the Sheriff Courts 23
in Scotland

LATIN TERMS

Some common Latin terms used in law

Amicus curiae . . . . a friend of the court
Cadit quaestio . . . . the issue cannot be argued further
Contra bonos mores . . . . against good morals
De jure . . . . by right
In delicto . . . . at fault
Ipsissima verba . . . . a speaker's actual words
In loco parentis . . . . in the place of a parent
In terrorem. . . . . as warning
In mala fides . . . . in bad faith
Onus probandi. . . . . burden of proof
Talis quails . . . . such as it is
Uno flatu . . . . in one breath

WEIRD LAWS AROUND THE WORLD

Singapore

Unless it is used as foreplay, oral sex is illegal.

The sale of gum is illegal, although chewing it is not, unless you are on the local transport system. The fines for leaving gum on the street are significant.

Other civic crimes include smoking in public buildings, littering, spitting, jaywalking, feeding birds in public places and failing to flush public lavatories. You can be fined on the spot for these offences, and you can be caned for not flushing; special police do random checks in public toilets.

You may not walk around in the nude at home if you are 'exposed to public view'. The fine is $2,000 or imprisonment for three months. Moreover, you can also fall foul of the law if you are dressed 'in such a manner as to offend against public decency or order'.

WHAT'S A COP?

Many different origins have been suggested for the word 'cop', a slang term for policeman, but the truth is that it is a shortening of 'copper', a word that is still used to refer to a police officer. The verb 'to cop', meaning 'to capture', was first used around 1700, and it was in use as a noun by the mid-1800s. 'To cop', meaning 'to catch', is related to the Dutch 'kapen', meaning 'to take'. Ultimately, the word is derived from the Latin capere – 'to capture'. There is less credence in the theory that it refers to a copper badge or copper buttons on a policeman's uniform.

---

24 *Age of Gwynne Owen Evans when she became one of the last two people to be executed in the UK on 13 August 1964*

QUOTE UNQUOTE

To succeed in other trades, capacity must be shown;
in the law, concealment will do.
Mark Twain, American novelist and humorist

FAMOUS LAWYERS

Robert Aske

When Henry VIII, who ruled England from 1509 to 1547, found himself in need of a male heir, he decided to divorce his first wife, Catalina de Aragon. However, when the Catholic church refused to allow the divorce, Henry broke with Rome and founded the Church of England, with himself at its head. He proceeded to force Catholic monks and nuns from their monasteries and nunneries. His extraordinary actions caused a rebellion called the Pilgrimage of Grace, a religious uprising in the north of England, extending over five counties and finding support across all parts of the country. The uprising was led by Robert Aske, who was a lawyer and a soldier in Henry's army.

When Henry began to close monasteries near Aske's home in East Yorkshire, Aske led a rebellion of over 30,000 pilgrims against Henry's Reformation. The protesters were so numerous that the king had to listen. At Doncaster the royal leaders, the Duke of Norfolk and the Earl of Shrewsbury, negotiated with Aske and his gathered supporters. They promised a pardon and a parliament to be held at York within one year. Trusting in the royal word, Aske dismissed his pilgrims. But Henry had no intention of keeping these promises. Robert Aske and his key leaders were subsequently arrested. They and over 150 of their followers were executed in July 1537.

CRIME WAVE

According to Interpol, the countries with the highest reported number of crimes in 2002, per 100,000 people, in descending order are:
1. Iceland
2. Sweden
3. New Zealand
4. Grenada
5. Norway
6. England and Wales
7. Denmark
8. Finland
9. Scotland
10. Canada

Years in prison that can be imposed for cutting down the rare Saguaro cactus 25
in Arizona

Dickens' character Tom Pinch has an office to himself in Middle Temple. Here the author describes the chambers where Tom is to work as a librarian.

There was a ghostly air about these uninhabited chambers in the Temple, and attending every circumstance of Tom's employment there, which had a strange charm in it. Every morning when he shut his door at Islington, he turned his face towards an atmosphere of unaccountable fascination, as surely as he turned it to the London smoke; and from that moment it thickened round and round him all day long, until the time arrived for going home again, and leaving it, like a motionless cloud, behind.

It seemed to Tom, every morning, that he approached this ghostly mist, and became enveloped in it, by the easiest succession of degrees imaginable. Passing from the roar and rattle of the streets into the quiet court-yards of the Temple, was the first preparation. Every echo of his footsteps sounded to him like a sound from the old walls and pavements, wanting language to relate the histories of the dim, dismal rooms; to tell him what lost documents were decaying in forgotten corners of the shut-up cellars, from whose lattices such mouldy sighs came breathing forth as he went past; to whisper of dark bins of rare old wine bricked up in vaults among the old foundations of the Halls; or mutter in a lower tone yet darker legends of the cross-legged knights, whose marble effigies were in the church. With the first planting of his foot upon the staircase of his dusty office, all these mysteries increased; until, ascending step by step, as Tom ascended, they attained their full growth in the solitary labours of the day.

Charles Dickens, *Martin Chuzzlewit*

QUOTE UNQUOTE

Laws can discover sin, but not remove it.
John Milton, poet

SONGS ABOUT THE LAW

A few songs concerning legal matters:
The Law – Ronny Jordan
Love is the Law – Sea Horses
Living With the Law – Chris Whitley
I Fought the Law and the Law Won – The Clash
Unjust – Zuvuya
Love is the Law – Harvey's Rabbit
Law of Things – The Bats
I Shot the Sheriff – Bob Marley

Sikhism

Sikhism was started in Punjab, an area that straddles India and Pakistan, by Guru Nanak Dev over 500 years ago. Its followers number 20 million throughout the world. 'Sikh' is taken from the Sanskrit word meaning 'disciple'. The key beliefs are that one should work hard and live honestly in order to gain positive karma. Karma is the effects of your actions – how well one lives determines how well you will live in your next, reincarnated life. Sikhs do not believe in ritual for its own sake or as a way to goodness, but believe in doing practical, good deeds on a day-to-day basis. Sikh men wear beards and turbans, but what is really important is not this outward sign of faith but the internal relationship with the one God. Sikhs believe in living in communities where everyone is equal. Sikhism may have originated, in part, as a reaction against the caste system in India.

LEGAL TEASERS

Question to a high fee-charging barrister:
Can I ask you to answer two legal questions for £300?
Answer on page 153

BEDLAM OR BETHLEHEM?

The word 'bedlam', referring to a noisy or confused place or mad-house, originates from a priory opened in London in 1247 for the order of St Mary of Bethlehem. It was founded by Simon Fitz Mary in Bishopsgate Street, now the site of Liverpool Street station. By the 1300s, the priory was used as a hospital, and at least some of the patients were insane. It was increasingly associated with the mad and the criminally insane, although some criminals of sound mind, at least initially, also found themselves interned. At various times in its history there were allegations that inmates were being abused, and in the 1700s the hospital became popular as a place to visit for the well-to-do with time on their hands. The admission charge was one penny and visits became so popular that the hospital made a tidy annual sum in this way. A number of the more fortunate inmates were discharged and licensed to beg. They were known as 'bedlamers' or 'bedlamites' and could be identified by a metal plate on their arm. Bedlam moved premises a number of times – to Finsbury Circus, then to St George's Fields (on the site of a madhouse of a different kind, the disreputable Dog and Duck Tavern) and finally to what is now the Imperial War Museum – before it was moved out of London altogether in 1930.

*If you want to get ahead in the legal profession,
stay on track with the news and get a good training.*

DEVIL'S DICTIONARY

Ambrose Bierce was an American writer and journalist. In his *Devil's Dictionary*, written in 1911, he lists the following legal definitions:

Appeal, *n.* In law, to put the dice into the box for another throw.

Lawful, *adj.* Compatible with the will of a judge having jurisdiction.

Lawyer, *n.* One skilled in circumvention of the law.

Litigant, *n.* A person about to give up his skin for the hope of retaining his bones.

Litigation, *n.* A machine which you go into as a pig and come out of as a sausage.

---

28 *The number of parking fines in the UK earned by diplomatic missions that remained unpaid last year*

LITERATURE AND THE LAW

There are countless civilised people who would shrink from murder or incest but who do not deny themselves the satisfaction of their avarice, their aggressive urges or their sexual lusts, and who do not hesitate to injure other people by lies, fraud and calumny, so long as they can remain unpunished for it; and this, no doubt, has always been so through many ages of civilisation.

Sigmund Freud, *The Future of an Illusion*

FAMOUS LAWYERS

Lord Denning

Lord Denning, Master of the Rolls (1899-1999) was a hugely influential judge renowned for using his cases to change the law when justice required. He was the greatest law-making judge of the 1900s and also the most controversial. He was called to the bar in 1923, rose rapidly through the ranks and was appointed to the Court of Appeal and then the House of Lords in 1957. He made his biggest impact when he stepped down to the position of Master of the Rolls in 1962. Lord Denning saw the judge's role as being proactive, making case law in defiance of legislation as necessary. 'Parliament does it too late. It may take years and years before a statute can be passed to amend a bad law,' he said. He championed the underdog and he shaped the common law to his own vision of society, evidenced by his attempts to establish an abandoned wives' equity fund, and to define the law regarding public authority liability. Though he had his critics, and perhaps stood as an example of the dangers of one man having too much power in that he effectively overruled legislation when he felt like it, he left an impressive legacy of cases. He stood for 'freedom under the law', a phrase of his own making, which was the way he liked it.

BUT I DIDN'T MEAN TO KILL HER...

In 1943 in England, a man found his girlfriend drinking with another man, N, with whom she was having an affair. The man went away and returned later with a cut-throat razor. He said that it was only his intention to scare N. However, his girlfriend, a little unsteady on her feet from too many drinks, fell against him and her throat was cut. She died.

The judge, in finding him guilty of murder, stated the difference between death following a lawful act and death following an unlawful act. Death that follows a lawful act may be manslaughter. But waving a sharp razor around is an unlawful act, and therefore the man was guilty of murdering his girlfriend, regardless of his intention.

*Number of codes which, together with the State Constitution and Statutes, 29
make up Californian Law*

The State of the City of the Vatican is the world's smallest independent country, both in size and population. It is where the Pope lives and forms the Holy See, the centre of authority for the Roman Catholic Church. Up until the mid-1800s, the Church had a number of papal states, which were territories over which the Pope had civil and spiritual authority. Most were taken over when the disparate parts of Italy united in the 1800s, leaving only Rome under papal control until it too was annexed in 1870 by Victor Emmanuel's army. Following an uneasy relationship between the Vatican and Italy, the Lateran treaties were signed in February 1929 between the Italian state and the Vatican, which was declared an independent state.

It consists mainly of St Peter's Basilica, the Sistine Chapel, the Vatican museums and St Peter's Square, all surrounded by the city wall. Its area is less than half a square kilometre, the population is 890, the currency is the euro, which replaced the Vatican lira in 2002, and Latin is the official language. As the government of the Catholic Church, the Holy See is considered to be a legal personality and as such it can sign treaties as much as any state can. The legal system is based on canon law, a body of codified laws governing the affairs of the Catholic Church; and the Pope, while effectively being an elected monarch, leaves the governing of the Vatican to the Pontifical Commission for the State of the Vatican City.

Two codes of canon law have been published, in 1917 and 1983. The legal system, based on canon law, includes courts and lawyers, with a Doctor of Canon Law being the highest office of learning in canon law. The 1983 Code of Canon Law lists penalties which the Church may inflict on the Christian faithful, including medicinal penalties or censures, or expiatory penalties. The latter can be imposed on a person for a limited time, an indeterminate time, or perpetually, and can determine where a person does or doesn't live; or it might be a privation of office, or dismissal from the clerical state. For example, a cleric can incur a suspension for the crime of falsehood; or an appropriate penalty can be imposed on a person for blasphemy, gravely injuring good morals, or exciting hatred or contempt against religion or the Church.

British Black Metal band Cradle of Filth found themselves on the receiving end of Vatican justice in 1999 when they walked into the Vatican State wearing T-shirts bearing an obscene legend. They were arrested, marched off at gunpoint and subjected to an interrogation before being ejected from the country.

30 *Number of days allowed under Roman law for a debtor to pay his debts, after which a creditor could imprison him*

COMING OF AGE

A brief guide to what you can legally do at what age in the UK

You can	Age
Open a building society account if the manager consents	10
Be convicted for a criminal offence	10
Buy particular pets	12
Get a part-time job	13
Be detained in a care home for 72 hours if you might injure yourself or others	13
Go into a pub and drink low-alcohol beer	14
Leave school	16
Leave home	16
Get a full-time job	16
Get a passport	16
Change your name by deed poll	16
Drive a car	17
Be sent to prison	17
Be a street trader	17
Make a will	18
Place a bet	18
Vote	18
See your birth certificate if you're adopted	18

QUOTE UNQUOTE

Whenever men take the law into their own hands, the loser is the law. And when the law loses, freedom languishes
Robert Francis Kennedy, US attorney general and advisor

SCHOOL'S OUT FOR EVER

The Columbine High School shooting in April 1999 is perhaps the most famous school shooting. To a large degree this is a result of Michael Moore's documentary about gun control, *Bowling for Columbine*, and Gus van Sant's Palme d'Or-winning film, *Elephant*, which was based on the events at the school. In the UK, the shootings at Dunblane Primary School are at least as prominent in the public mind. Although the highest death toll for murders in a school were at Dunblane and Columbine, where 16 students and one teacher and 14 students and one teacher were killed respectively, since 1996 there have been numerous shootings by students or former students in 37 schools throughout the world. In these attacks, 72 students were killed and 134 injured, and 33 teachers were killed and seven injured. The youngest victim was six years old, as was the youngest killer. Of the 37 incidents, only nine occurred outside the USA.

*Number of lawyers among the 412 Labour MPs when they were re-elected 31
in Britain in 2001*

DRUG USE AND THE FAMOUS

Drug use among the famous has been with us for a long time. Here are a few of the harder drugs that have been used, often in contravention of the law, and the famous people who favoured them:

Heroin
John Belushi, actor (died under its influence); William Burroughs, writer; Lenny Bruce, comedian; Kurt Cobain, musician; Jimi Hendrix, musician (died under its influence); Billie Holiday, musician; River Phoenix, actor (died under its influence).

LSD
Isaac Abrams, artist; Peter Fonda, actor; Larry Hagman, actor; Aldous Huxley, writer; Ken Kesey, writer; Timothy Leary, philosopher; Kary Mullis, Nobel Prize Winner in chemistry.

Cocaine
Sarah Bernhardt, actress; Robert Downey Jr, actor; Sigmund Freud, psychologist; King George V; Cole Porter, musician; Elvis Presley, singer and actor.

Opium
Marcus Aurelius, Roman emperor; Elizabeth Barrett Browning, poet; Jean Cocteau, artist and writer; Arthur Conan Doyle, writer; William Gladstone, British prime minister; Joseph McCarthy, US senator.

THE LAW OF AVERAGES

The law of averages is the popular term for an idea based on Bernoulli's Law, or the Law of Large Numbers, which is a mathematical theorem. Jakob Bernoulli (1654-1705) came from a Swiss family of mathematicians and his work included the development of the calculus of variations. His law of averages says, quite simply, that everything will average out in the end. It supposes that there are an equal number of likely events in the world and if some of them have happened already, then it is more likely that the remaining ones will happen. However, the law of averages is not strictly correct. For example, if someone flips a coin 50 times and gets tails every time, you might think on the law of averages that they are more likely to get heads on the next flip. This is false. There is a 50/50 chance each time and the person is no more likely to get heads on flip number 51 than they were on flip number one. Under the Law of Large Numbers, the more times you flip a coin the closer the average will get to the underlying probability though the absolute deviation will increase. For example, the more times you flip a coin the greater the probability will tend toward 50/50, but there will be a greater number of variations between heads or tails (absolute deviation). In this sense the law of averages is false – deviation will always increase so things will not always 'average out'.

WORLD'S FIRST SPEEDING TICKET

Walter Arnold had the ignominy, or perhaps the fame, of being the first person in the world to be given a speeding ticket. Mr Arnold was pulled over and arrested in Paddock Wood, Kent in January 1896. How did he get caught? He was racing past a policeman's cottage and caught the attention of the officer who hotly pursued him on a bicycle. The speed? Mr Arnold was charged with driving at eight miles per hour in a two miles per hour zone. He received a fine of one shilling. Three years later the first speeding ticket was issued in the US. Jacob German was arrested in New York City after being caught speeding at 12 miles per hour in an electric taxi. However, in the light of modern traffic congestion, it is unlikely that anyone would reach such dangerous speeds in New York City today.

COPS ON TV

Starsky and Hutch (1975-79)
Hill Street Blues (1981-87)
Cagney & Lacey (1982-88)
Miami Vice (1984-89)
The Bill (1983-)
Dixon of Dock Green (1955-76)
Z Cars (1962-78)
The Sweeney (1975-78)
Cracker (1993-96)
Kojak (1973-1978)
A Touch of Frost (1992-2004)
Remington Steele (1982-87)
Heartbeat (1992-)

LAWYERS WHO FELL FOUL OF THE LAW

George Morton Levy was a US lawyer who started his career in Freeport, Maine in 1912. After a shaky start, he successfully defended a number of murder cases, particularly of women who had killed cheating husbands and lovers. After this, he began to defend bigger fish, men on the edge of organised crime, like James Brown and Dubert L Armstrong. In 1935 he defended Charles 'Lucky' Luciano for trafficking prostitutes. Despite an impressive performance protecting the gangster, Lucky went down for 30 to 60 years, leaving the public appalled at the details of his prostitution rackets. Levy handed over the appeal at that stage. However, from that time he was always known as Lucky Luciano's lawyer, and his reputation was forever tainted for being a mob lawyer.

JOHN GRISHAM NOVELS
ON THE BIG SCREEN

The Firm (1993)
Tom Cruise plays the hot new lawyer fresh out of law school who unwittingly accepts a job at a law firm in Memphis controlled by the mob.

The Pelican Brief (1993)
Julia Roberts is the spunky law student who has her conspiracy theory vindicated when her boss is murdered by a hitman. Denzel Washington is the crusading lawyer who helps her along the way.

Rainmaker (1997)
Matt Damon stars as the idealistic young lawyer taking on a big corporate health insurance firm and falling in love with Claire Danes along the way.

The Client (1994)
Susan Sarandon is the lawyer who represents a young boy who knows too much after he witnesses the suicide and final confession of a lawyer for a mobster.

The Chamber (1996)
Chris O'Donnell is a new lawyer who takes on his grandfather's case, just four weeks before the grandfather, played by Gene Hackman, is due to be executed for the murder of two young Jewish boys 30 years before. The rookie lawyer takes the case despite his grandfather's links to the Ku Klux Klan.

A Time to Kill (1996)
Matthew McConaughey is the young lawyer who takes on the case of a black man who shot dead two white men who raped his 10-year-old daughter.

The Gingerbread Man (1998)
A young lawyer, Kenneth Branagh, takes on the case of a young woman who is having problems with her violent father.

Runaway Jury (2003)
Dustin Hoffman and Gene Hackman battle for the verdict they want from the jury in a landmark case against the gun lobby. However, one man on the jury has his own agenda.

Which film is the odd one out?
Answer: *The Gingerbread Man* – this story by Grisham was actually never published.

QUOTE UNQUOTE

The best laws cannot make a constitution work in spite of morals; morals can turn the worst laws to advantage.
That is a commonplace truth, but one to which my studies are always bringing me back. It is the central point in my conception.
I see it at the end of all my reflections.
Alexis de Tocqueville, French political writer

34 *Age of the youngest judge ever appointed to a US Court of Appeals when he was commissioned in 1892*

THE COMMONS CORRIDOR

Were you to walk down the Commons Corridor in the British House of Commons, you would observe eight paintings by EM Ward depicting events from the Stuart Period. On the west side, concerning events from 1685 to 1689, you would see:

1. Alice Lisle, hiding fugitives after the Battle of Sedgemoor.
2. The Earl of Argyll sleeping peacefully, despite the fact that he is about to be executed for trying to liberate Scotland.
3. William and Mary being offered the Crown at Whitehall.
4. The acquittal of the seven bishops who refused to read James II's Declaration of Indulgence.

On the east side, concerning events from 1650 to 1660, you would see:

1. Charles II on the run after the Battle of Worcester.
2. Montrose being led to his death.
3. Charles II arriving at Dover.
4. The declaration of a free parliament by General Monck.

LEGAL QUANDARIES

Fifty men are in freezing water in danger of drowning. However, there is a ladder to safety. One man called X, frozen in fear, is on the ladder blocking the escape route. Another man called Y, after yelling at him for 10 minutes, pushes him off the ladder into the water and he is never seen again. The others climb to safety. Is Y guilty of murdering X?

Answer on page 153

NOTORIOUS PRISONS

Alcatraz

Alcatraz Prison, or 'The Rock' as it was known, still exists on Alcatraz Island in San Francisco Bay, though now as a tourist attraction rather than a penitentiary. It was originally a military fortress-cum-disciplinary-barracks before becoming a federal prison in 1934. It housed a number of famous criminals including the gangster Al Capone. The prison was proud of the fact that no one had ever escaped – or at least they didn't survive the attempt. In June 1964 three prisoners did escape from their cells but were never seen nor heard of again. Their escape attempt was dramatised in the movie *Escape from Alcatraz*. In the film, Clint Eastwood plays Frank Morris, one of the missing prisoners, and of course Clint has to get away, but it is presumed that in reality the escapees drowned. Then again, they would have had good reasons to lay low and never be heard from again. The prison closed in 1963 for financial reasons.

LITERATURE AND THE LAW

There are, still, worse places than the Temple, on a sultry day, for basking in the sun, or resting idly in the shade. There is yet a drowsiness in its courts, and a dreamy dullness in its trees and gardens; those who pace its lanes and squares may yet hear the echoes of their footsteps on the sounding stones, and read upon its gates, in passing from the tumult of the Strand or Fleet Street, 'Who enters here leaves noise behind'. There is still the splash of falling water in fair Fountain Court, and there are yet nooks and corners where dun-haunted students may look down from their dusty garrets, on a vagrant ray of sunlight patching the shade of the tall houses, and seldom troubled to reflect a passing stranger's form. There is yet, in the Temple, something of a clerkly monkish atmosphere, which public offices of law have not disturbed, and even legal firms have failed to scare away. In summer time, its pumps suggest to thirsty idlers, springs cooler, and more sparkling, and deeper than other wells; and as they trace the spillings of full pitchers on the heated ground, they snuff the freshness, and, sighing, cast sad looks towards the Thames, and think of baths and boats, and saunter on, despondent.

Charles Dickens, *Barnaby Rudge*

LEGAL MUSICIANS

John Law & Louis Moholo –
The Boat is Sinking, Apartheid is Sinking
Law & Order – *Rites of Passage*
Down By Law – *Fly the Flag*
Tramlaw – *Law of Averages*
Leash Law – *Dogface*
Lisa Law – *Fall at Your Feet*
The Law – *Laying Down the Law*

TWENTY-EIGHT SECONDS OF TERROR

Passengers on an American Airlines flight from LA to New York in 1995 feared for their lives when they were hurled from their seats after the plane hit turbulence. The flight had run into a thunderstorm and 28 seconds of chaos ensued. The plane rose and fell a number of times and then dived as if it had lost power. When the passengers brought a lawsuit against American Airlines for psychological injury, the jury found in their favour. While it might seem unfair to blame the airline for bad weather, it emerged that they had been warned of the storm but failed to turn on the seatbelt sign. The passengers were awarded a total of $2 million.

The legal wig has long been a distinctive feature of the English barrister, and is still used in over 20 former colonies. The origin of the wig lies in France, during the reign of Louis XIII in the early seventeenth century. Louis XIII went prematurely bald, and to disguise it, he started wearing a wig. Being the king and a noted paragon of style, he started a fashion which continued when his son, Louis XIV, also suffered from a swiftly receding hairline. The habit arrived in England when King Charles II, another style icon with a bald spot, returned to the throne from exile in France in 1660. Soon upper-class and middle-class men all over Europe were wearing wigs made from horse hair, yak hair and human hair, which was the most expensive. Ede & Ravenscroft, maker of legal wigs, was established in 1689 and today is still England's leading wigmaker.

Wigmakers used powder to make the colour of bleached wigs stable. The powder was usually white and made from ground starch scented with lavender, orange flower or orris root. A tax on powder in England in 1795 meant the end of the wig heyday, and its association with the aristocracy in France saw its demise there during the French Revolution. However, lawyers and judges continued to wear them, and the tradition continues to this day.

Barristers wear 'tie wigs', judges the bigger 'bob wigs' and barristers, judges and the House of Lords wear the longer 'spaniel wigs' on special occasions. Wigs range in price from £400 to £3,000, but even for £3,000 you won't get a human hair wig – white horsehair is now used, which itself replaced black horsehair to reflect the fashion of lighter-coloured wigs from about 1715.

Curiously, there is no law governing the use of wigs. The last decree concerning court attire was the Judicial Rules of 1635, before the arrival of the wig in England. So now solicitor advocates, who can speak in court but don't wear a wig, are calling for the right to wear it, as juries appear to be influenced by the gravitas that a wig affords. The wig seems set to stay, despite debates about whether it should be abandoned altogether. Complaints by judges include that the wig is unsanitary, too hot and ridiculous in appearance. The Lord Chancellor of England, Lord Irvine of Lairg, even asked permission of the House of Lords in 1999 to take his wig off when sitting. Naturally the Lords had to vote on it. They granted his request – 145 to 115 in favour.

LODZ OF MONEY

In 2004 police officers in Lodz in Poland were told that they would get a bonus for every criminal caught. An arrest for the average criminal nets an officer 200 zlotys (about £30) and up to 700 zlotys (about £110) is awarded for catching a more serious criminal. The police chief, Aldona Kostrzewoya, said she initiated the scheme when only six criminals a day were being caught despite an average 90 crimes per day being reported. 'The scheme is just like any other motivational programme in a normal company,' she explained. The number of average arrests has tripled since the scheme came into force.

LEGALLY MARRIED

I take this woman...

Around 200 AD the Germanic Goths had a very direct approach to courtship. As a good woman was hard to find, it fell to the average male Goth to get off his behind and go and get one. This involved riding into a neighbouring village, quickly scanning for any nubile young women who had strayed too far from their parental home, and throwing one on his horse and taking her back to his village for a shotgun marriage – or, rather, a clubs, knives and swords marriage, which were kept under the altar to protect against the possibility of the fiancée being snatched back by her upset family. Indeed, the tradition of a best man sprang from the fact that raiding a village for a wife was a hazardous pursuit and one that required a tasty sidekick for back-up. The snatch-and-run method of acquiring a wife also inspired the tradition of carrying a bride across the threshold. During the ceremony itself the woman stood to the left of the man so he could keep his sword hand free to dispatch any relatives who turned up to the ceremony uninvited.

IN A BIT OF A PICKLE

According to the *Charlestown Daily Mail*, a convenience store worker in West Virginia sued after she sustained a back injury while opening a jar of pickles. What was surprising was not so much that she won, but the amount she was awarded: US$2.2 million. At least one of the judges thought this extravagant. Justice Spike Maynard of the State Supreme Court called the award outrageous. 'I know an excessive punitive damages award when I see one, and I see one here,' he wrote. However, his opinion was dissenting (meaning it differed to the other judges). The award was made for punitive damages, compensation and emotional distress.

38 *Height in inches of a man who filed suit in 2001 demanding that dwarf-tossing be re-legalised in Florida following his loss of income*

An unfortunate moment of impromptu deshabille for the highwayman, and the phrase 'Stick 'em up' was born.

HEAVY METAL BANDS AND THE LAW

For the self-professed outlaws of music, they sure seem to be obsessed with the law. Here are a few of the heavy metal bands who have made albums about the law:

Saxon – *Strong Arm of the Law*
4 Skins – *One Law for Them*
Hate Plow – *The Only Law is Survival*
Stryper – *Against the Law*
Judas Priest – *Breaking the Law*
Genitorturers – *Flesh is the Law*
Annihilator – *Law*
Neurosis – *Word As Law*
Ritual Carnage – *Highest Law*
Heaven Shall Burn – *In Battle There is No Law*

Question: Spot the odd one out.
Answer: Stryper are a Christian heavy metal band.

TURNING THE SCREWS

The slang term for a prison officer is a 'screw'. The term originates with a machine called The Crank, which was a device used as a punishment. A handle turned a wheel inside The Crank. Resistance to turning the handle was controlled either by sand or gravel in the box, or by a brake which was controlled by a screw. Tightening the screw meant the handle was harder to turn. The punishment involved turning the handle for as long as the warder – the screw – dictated. The average number of turns per minute was 20, and as the required number of turns could be as many as 10,000, the punishment could be a long and demoralising one. Another contributing factor is that from at least 1795 'screw' was also slang for a key – the object that ensures a prisoner remains confined.

MOST COMMON OFFENCES IN ENGLAND AND WALES

The following were the most common offences
in England and Wales in 2002:

Theft and handling stolen goods (excluding car theft)	1,363,500
Criminal damage	1,089,500
Car theft (including theft from vehicles)	998,400
Violation against a person	742,900
Burglary (non-domestic)	463,300
Domestic burglary	447,100
Fraud and forgery	326,300
Drug offences	130,200
Robbery	120,700
Sexual offences	45,700

LITERATURE AND THE LAW

Judges must beware of hard constructions and strained inferences, for there is no worse torture than the torture of laws. Specially in case of laws penal, they ought to have care that that which was meant for terror be not turned into rigour; and that they bring not upon the people that shower whereof the Scripture speaketh, *Pluet super eos laqueos* [*'They are a shower of snares on the people'*]; for penal laws pressed are a shower of snares upon the people. Therefore let penal laws, if they have been sleepers of long, or if they be grown unfit for the present time, be by wise judges confined in the execution: *Judicis officium est, ut res, ita tempora rerum* [*'It is a judge's duty to consider not only the circumstances, but also the time of an act'*], etc. In causes of life and death, judges ought in justice to remember mercy, and to cast a severe eye upon the example, but a merciful eye upon the person.

Francis Bacon, *Of Judicature*

40 *Fine, in pounds, for fishing without a rod licence in the UK*

IGNORANCE OF THE LAW IS NO DEFENCE

As you travel the world you may find yourself falling foul of the law without even realising. For the benefit of the international traveller, here, in no particular order, are some of the laws to be aware of:

- It is illegal to farm pigs in Israel.
- Oklahoma prohibits wine sales on Independence Day, Memorial Day, Labour Day, Thanksgiving and Christmas.
- In Colorado, half-bottles of wine are illegal.
- In Lee County, Alabama it is illegal to sell peanuts after dark on a Wednesday. However, in Lee County you can drive the wrong way down a one-way street on condition that you have a lantern attached to your vehicle.
- In Lavadou, France it is against the law to die unless you have already bought yourself a grave site. It is unclear how those who break this law are punished. At any rate, as a visitor, this law ought not to apply to you but, please, take care.

QUOTE UNQUOTE

The precepts of the law are these:
To live honorably, not to injure another, to give each his due.
Justinian, Byzantine Emperor

WHO ARE YOU CALLING A PIG?

The origin of the word 'pig' as slang for a police officer dates back as far as the 1540s, when there weren't many policemen, but the word was used to refer to a despicable person. It was hundreds of years later before it was applied specifically to an officer of the law. *The Lexicon Balatronicum* (1811) refers to a member of the Bow Street Runners, one of the prototype police forces of London, as a 'China Street Pig'. The same document refers to the saying 'floor the pig and bolt', meaning punching out a policeman's lights and making a run for it. The term fell out of use but returned in the 1960s in America with the Vietnam War protests. One suggestion is the use of gas marks made police look like pigs to protesters. Another possibility is that the use by the British army of a lightly-armoured vehicle, called a 'pig', for crowd control in Northern Ireland made the jump to calling an officer 'pig' an easy one. At any rate, 'pig' was an old nickname for the police, but one which only returned into fashion in the 1960s. If you're in any doubt about its continuing popularity, listen to any record by American superstar rappers Cypress Hill.

RA RA, RASPUTIN

When MGM made the 1932 movie *Rasputin and the Empress*, aka *Rasputin the Mad Monk*, about the Siberian peasant monk who infamously held sway over Russia's Tsarina Alexandra, they thought better of using the name Prince Yusupov. The real Prince Yusupov was a Russian nobleman noted for his role in the death of Rasputin in 1916. MGM decided instead to call their character Prince Chegodieff. Yet Yusupov still sued MGM in a London court and was awarded a sizeable amount of money. To add insult to injury, MGM were sued again shortly after and had to pay out a substantial amount again – this time to the real Prince Chegodieff.

DIVINE ASSISTANCE

Even lawyers have patron saints to help them

Alphonsus Liguori . . . . , patron saint of confessors
Barbara . . . . patron saint of prisoners
Dismas . . . . patron saint of prisoners (they need more than one)
Genesius . . . . patron saint of lawyers
Ivo . . . . .patron saint of lawyers
(they also need more than one)
John Capistran . . . . patron saint of jurists
John Nepomucen . . . . patron saint of confessors
Joseph Cafasso . . . . patron saint of prisons
Matthew . . . . patron saint of tax collectors
Michael . . . . patron saint of policemen
Raymond Nonnatus . . . . patron saint of the falsely accused
Thomas More . . . . patron saint of lawyers (three should do it)

THE BEATING OF THE BOUNDS

The beating of the bounds is a custom that was widespread during medieval times in England and has existed for about 2,000 years. It played an important role in reinforcing charters, which were legal documents prescribing property rights. During the ceremony, the priest and parishioners walk the boundaries of a parish with long thin sticks of birch or willow to mark out, or beat, the perimeters, saying prayers at certain places on the way. The ceremony usually used to take place on Ascension Day, and in addition to beating the bounds with sticks to remember where they were, boys were sometimes pushed into walls or hit with sticks to remind them of the boundaries or were hung upside-down and had their head knocked against marker stones. The procession itself continues as a custom to this day. However, hanging children upside-down and bashing their heads against rock is no longer considered necessary.

For almost 700 years the samurai were the law in Japan. A ruling class of warriors with humble beginnings as militiamen and royal guards at the court in Kyoto, the samurai took power in 1185 and made themselves into a ruling elite whose law was imposed by force.

A samurai ('one who serves') wore a kimono under flowing trousers and a short jacket, shaved his head on top and grew his hair long at the sides and back, securing it in a top knot. He was armed with two swords, one long, one short, and was loyal to a warlord. As the warlords grew more powerful, the Emperor became a mere figurehead and the samurai leader, the shogun, who was effectively a military dictator, was the real leader. The first shogun was Yorimoto, the leader of the Minamoto clan, who wielded his power from the fishing village of Kamakura, now a suburb of Tokyo.

Although the samurai were originally horsemen who specialised in archery, the two Mongol Wars in the 1200s and the hand-to-hand combat that the samurai were forced into ushered in the era of the sword. In both wars, fierce storms helped the samurai to defeat the forces of Kublai Khan, grandson of Ghenghis Khan, who attacked from the sea. Both storms disabled the Mongol ships and the second storm was named the kamikaze – the 'divine wind'. The Japanese suicide pilots of World War II took their inspiration from this storm.

Headhunting was one of the more bloody aspects of being a samurai. Heads of fallen enemies were presented to warlords after battle and warriors were rewarded accordingly. In a similarly bloodthirsty fashion, samurai facing defeat would commit hara-kiri or seppuku – death by disembowelment – rather than be captured. On the other hand, samurai also indulged in quieter arts such as flower arranging and poetry, and most were devout Buddhists.

In 2004 Japan celebrated the 400th anniversary of the start of the Edo Period (1603-1867), which encompassed both the height of the samurai power and its downfall. One factor in the downfall was the 250-year peace of the Tokugawa shoguns. With no wars to be fought, many samurai lost their fighting edge and merely enjoyed their status as the upper class, with farmers, artisans and merchants in descending class order below them. As their military skill was dulled by peace, and even the lowest class of merchants overpowered them financially, the end was in sight. When American warships entered Japan, and it was clear the shogun could not effectively defend Japan, forces loyal to the new emperor rose up and defeated the shogun's army in 1867, at the same time finishing the extraordinary reign of the samurai.

Felonies.

CLEANLINESS AND THE LAW

Before a law was passed in 1978 requiring dog owners in New York City to clean up after their dogs, it was estimated that 40 million pounds of dog excrement were deposited on the streets every year.

In Kentucky, every citizen is required to have a bath at least once a year. In Portland, Oregon it is illegal to urinate while on roller-skates.

In the US, an 1899 Federal Statute made it illegal to dump any industrial waste into any body of water.

Last but not least, for laws about the personal purity of priests, see the Book of Leviticus 21:5 in the Bible: 'They shall not make tonsures upon their heads, nor shave off the edges of their beards, nor make any cuttings in their flesh.'

Revenge is a kind of wild justice, which the more a man's nature runs to, the more ought law to weed it out.
Francis Bacon, writer

LITERATURE AND THE LAW

LUNARIAN: Then when your Congress has passed a law it goes directly to the Supreme Court in order that it may at once be known whether it is constitutional?

TERRESTRIAN: Oh no; it does not require the approval of the Supreme Court until having perhaps been enforced for many years somebody objects to its operation against himself – I mean his client. The President, if he approves it, begins to execute it at once.

LUNARIAN: Ah, the executive power is a part of the legislative. Do your policemen also have to approve the local ordinances that they enforce?

TERRESTRIAN: Not yet – at least not in their character of constables. Generally speaking, though, all laws require the approval of those whom they are intended to restrain.

LUNARIAN: I see. The death warrant is not valid until signed by the murderer.

TERRESTRIAN: My friend, you put it too strongly; we are not so consistent.

LUNARIAN: But this system of maintaining an expensive judicial machinery to pass upon the validity of laws only after they have long been executed, and then only when brought before the court by some private person – does it not cause great confusion?

TERRESTRIAN: It does.

LUNARIAN: Why then should not your laws, previously to being executed, be validated, not by the signature of your President, but by that of the Chief Justice of the Supreme Court?

TERRESTRIAN: There is no precedent for any such course.

LUNARIAN: Precedent. What is that?

TERRESTRIAN: It has been defined by 500 lawyers in three volumes each. So how can any one know?

Ambrose Bierce, *The Devil's Dictionary*

LEGAL QUANDARIES

Bob plans to murder his business partner, Bill, while Bill is asleep. He sneaks into his bedroom and shoots him six times, then leaves. Unbeknown to Bob, Bill died of a heart attack 15 minutes before Bob shot him. Is Bob guilty of murder?
Answer on page 153

COLOURFUL LAW

While some may complain that the law lacks colour, this is clearly not the case...

Blackmail: a crime where pressure is used to attempt to obtain money or favours, often by the threat of disclosing sensitive information about the blackmailed person. The term originates from Scotland where thieves would demand 'black mail' (illegal rent) from land owners to secure freedom from raids.

Black market: the organised, illegal buying and selling of goods.

Black Hole of Calcutta: a notorious prison in India into which in 1756, as the story goes, 143 prisoners were forced and only 23 survived.

Yellow-dog contract: In the US employers used this form of contract to forbid employees from joining a union and thereby to disrupt any union activity. Such contracts are now illegal. (The term 'yellow dog' refers to a mongrel or despicable person.)

Red Book of the Exchequer: This book was written in the thirteenth century as a record of matters relating to royal property and money owing by tenants, particularly for money owing in lieu of military service.

Red Mass: This annual mass marks the beginning of the judicial year. The red refers to the robes of the priests and judges. Celebrated in Europe since the thirteenth century, the Red Mass is now held in Westminster Cathedral and Westminster Abbey.

White-collar crime: crime relating to the professional occupations.

White Paper: A government report on a matter that is being considered as a subject for legislation. Typically, a government department will investigate all aspects of the matter in the White Paper and Parliament will consider it when debating the bill.

NOTORIOUS PRISONS

Robben Island

Robben Island ('robben' is Dutch for 'seal') was a maximum security prison and for 400 years it was used to isolate people, often political prisoners from South Africa and other Dutch colonies. From 1836 to 1931 it was a leper colony. However, it is most famous for being the prison where Nelson Mandela spent much of his 27 years of incarceration. It is no longer a prison but a museum and is considered to be a symbol of the power of the human spirit over adversity. It is also a World Heritage Site.

There is no flesh in man's obdurate heart,
It does not feel for man; the nat'ral bond
Of brotherhood is severed as the flax
That falls asunder at the touch of fire.
He finds his fellow guilty of a skin
Not coloured like his own; and, having pow'r
T' enforce the wrong, for such a worthy cause
Dooms and devotes him as his lawful prey.
Lands intersected by a narrow frith
Abhor each other. Mountains interposed
Make enemies of nations, who had else,
Like kindred drops, been mingled into one.
Thus man devotes his brother, and destroys;
And, worse than all, and most to be deplored,
As human nature's broadest, foulest blot,
Chains him, and tasks him, and exacts his sweat
With stripes, that mercy, with a bleeding heart,
Weeps when she sees inflicted on a beast.
Then what is man? And what man, seeing this,
And having human feelings, does not blush,
And hang his head, to think himself a man?

William Cowper, *Against Slavery*

AN ELOQUENT APPEAL

In the case of R v Blaue [1975] 3 All ER 446, a man, B, stabbed a girl who subsequently died after she refused to have a blood transfusion. It was argued that if she had accepted a transfusion, she would have survived, but the court found that B was guilty of manslaughter. In response to the argument that the girl's refusal was unreasonable, one of the judges, Lawton LJ, waxed lyrical about the subjective nature of such an assertion in the following terms: 'At once the question arises – reasonable by whose standards? Those of Jehovah's Witnesses? Humanists? Roman Catholics? Protestants of Anglo-Saxon descent? The man on the Clapham omnibus? But he might well be an admirer of Eleazar who suffered death rather than eat the flesh of swine [*see 2 Maccabees, ch 6, vv 18-31*] or of Sir Thomas More who, unlike nearly all his contemporaries, was unwilling to accept Henry VIII as Head of the Church in England. Those brought up in the Hebraic and Christian traditions would probably be reluctant to accept that these martyrs caused their own deaths.' Hard to argue with reasoning like that – B's appeal against his conviction for manslaughter was dismissed.

HIGHEST PRISON POPULATIONS

Country	Approx number imprisoned in 2004
1. United States	2 million
2. China	1.4 million
3. Russia	920,000
4. India	280,000
5. Brazil	230,000
6. Thailand	220,000
7. Ukraine	200,000
8. South Africa	180,000
9. Iran	160,000
10. Mexico	150,000
11. Rwanda	110,000
12. Kazakhstan	80,000

QUOTE UNQUOTE

Lawyers use the law as shoemakers use leather; rubbing it, pressing it, and stretching it with their teeth, all to the end of making it fit their purposes.
Louis XII, King of France

THE LEGALITY OF ONIONS

You may think nothing of deciding what it is you're going to eat for dinner. However, you need to be aware that you can't just go and eat anything you want, especially if you have a taste for onions, because in West Virginia it's illegal for children to have onion on their breath at school. However, it is legal to eat road-kill in West Virginia, a law passed to save money on road maintenance. (As far as we are aware, children are allowed to have road-kill on their breath at school – as long as it is not cooked with onions.) A minister may not eat onions or garlic before delivering a sermon in Marion, Oregon. In Waterloo, Nebraska a barber may not eat onions between 7am and 7pm. One can see the sense in that. But note that if you are in Hackberry, Arizona and you are a woman, you may not eat raw onions while drinking buttermilk on a Sunday – which is more difficult to understand. Enjoy your trip to Arizona, but bear in mind that it's illegal to hunt camels anywhere and it is also against the law to refuse to give someone a glass of water, unless perhaps they've been illegally eating onions. Then, of course, if a wife finds her husband drinking in Wolf Point, Montana, it is her moral, wifely duty to make him eat raw onions.

48 *Length, in inches, of Crime Scene Super Sticks, part of the Blood Splatter Kit 2000, used for blood splatter analysis at crime scenes*

There are two components normally required for a crime to be committed. *Mens rea* – the mental element or intention to commit a crime; and *actus reus* – the act itself that constitutes the crime.

However, there are occasions where this relatively straightforward formula doesn't quite fit. In the Privy Council case of Thabo Meli v R [1954] 1 All ER 373, the appellants led a man to a shed, gave him beer, then hit him over the head with the intention of killing him. They thought they had killed him so they took the body and rolled it down a hill to make it look like an accident. In fact, the man was still alive. However, lying unconscious at the bottom of the hill, he died later from exposure. The appellants argued that they were not guilty of murder because although they had the intention (*mens rea*) in the shed, they didn't succeed so the act (*actus reus*) was missing. When they rolled him down the hill they did not have the *mens rea*, believing him already dead, despite the *actus reus* being present.

The Privy Council took a dim view of this argument. They held that it was impossible to divide up what was really one series of acts. Although the law had not come across this exact situation before, they said that a person could not escape the penalties of the law because the *mens rea* and *actus reus* did not coincide in a situation such as this. They were found guilty.

LITERATURE AND THE LAW

Rene Descartes decided to follow a moral code 'composed of three or four maxims'. Here he describes the first:
The first was to obey the laws and customs of my country, adhering firmly to the faith in which, by the grace of God, I had been educated from my childhood and regulating my conduct in every other matter according to the most moderate opinions, and the farthest removed from extremes, which should happen to be adopted in practice with general consent of the most judicious of those among whom I might be living. For as I had from that time begun to hold my own opinions for nought because I wished to subject them all to examination, I was convinced that I could not do better than follow in the meantime the opinions of the most judicious; and although there are some perhaps among the Persians and Chinese as judicious as among ourselves, expediency seemed to dictate that I should regulate my practice conformably to the opinions of those with whom I should have to live.
Rene Descartes, *Discourse on the Method of Rightly Conducting the Reason, and Seeking Truth in the Sciences*

AGE OF CONSENT

The age of consent is the age at which the law allows people to agree to have sex. This can differ greatly from country to country and is not always clear. Here are a few examples of different countries and their laws for male-female, male-male and female-female sex.

Country	Male-Female	Male-Male	Female-Female
Albania	14	14	14
Algeria	16	Illegal	Illegal
Bahamas	16	18	18
Bulgaria	14	14	14
China	14	Not defined	Not defined
Costa Rica	15	15	15
Estonia	14	16	16
France	15	15	15
Germany	14	14	14
Guyana	13	Illegal	Illegal
Hungary	14	18	18
Indonesia	17	No laws	No laws
Japan	13	13	13
Korea	13	13	13
Madagascar	21	21	21
Malta	12	12	12
Netherlands	12	12	12
Oman	None	Illegal	Illegal
Pakistan	None	Illegal	Illegal
Romania	14	Illegal	Illegal
Saudi Arabia	Must be married	Illegal	Illegal
Swaziland	18	Illegal	Illegal
Taiwan	16	16	16
United Kingdom	16	16	16
Uzbekistan	16	Illegal	16
Zimbabwe	12	Illegal	Illegal

GRASS

The term 'grass' means to inform on somebody else, and is commonly associated with police informers who are part of the criminal fraternity, but who inform or 'grass' for financial gain or to lessen a penalty they face. The term comes from the Cockney rhyming slang for copper, which is grasshopper – hence 'grass' for someone who informs a copper. Alternatives include stoolie, stoolpigeon, canary, fink, squealer or rat.

50 *Number of pages, in thousands, of the official court transcript in the OJ Simpson trial*

LAWYERS WHO FELL FOUL OF THE LAW

George Avery took an unusual route to becoming a lawyer by beginning his law studies while in prison. He was up on a murder charge in 1870 when he escaped on the way to court because the sheriff was drunk. However, showing remarkable consideration for the officer who lost him, the following day he gave himself up to the hungover sheriff. Although acquitted of the murder charge, he served a year and a half for burglary, during which he began his legal studies. On release he went into practice in Philadelphia, although he later served another prison sentence for failing to pay a debt. He practised very successfully until he was convicted of forgery, for which he served almost five years, this time in the Western Penitentiary. Despite an offer to help him escape, made by the warden's daughter, who had fallen in love with the charismatic Avery, he declined, as by now he had found God. Despite his conversion, on his release he conned his neighbour out of $100 and fled under shotgun fire. In 1882 he opened another law practice, but at the same time struck it rich, to the tune of $750,000, speculating for gold. He then married the warden's daughter and lived happily ever after.

LEGAL QUANDARIES

X knocks out Y and leaves him unconscious on the floor of a building. Later an earthquake hits and the building collapses, killing Y. Is X guilty of murder?

Answer on page 153

ONE FOR THE BIRDS

In February 2004, Florida resident Edward Renna brought a small claims law suit against his neighbours, Chuck and Marian Butler. Their crime? Feeding the birds. Well, not just feeding them but feeding them 40 pounds of bird seed every week for years on end. Edward became so exasperated running around after birds in his garden and cleaning bird droppings off his boat that he felt justified in suing them. Edward chiefly wanted Chuck and Marian to stop feeding the birds, but he also couldn't resist asking for $5,000 for damage to his boat and fruit trees, and as recompense for the mental anguish he incurred while sweeping up avian poop. Unfortunately, Judge Peyton Hyslop seemed to feel that 'mental anguish' was taking things a bit far, and ruled that Ed had failed to prove Chuck and Marian were the sole source of the problem. Clearly Ed failed to meet the bird-en of proof.

Psalm read by convicts in the Middle Ages that entitled them to 'Benefit of 51 *Clergy', an escape from the death penalty*

Mary was so embarrassed. Here was Alfie giving it some, and road rage hadn't even been invented yet.

LITERATURE AND THE LAW

The greater the number of consequences resulting from any law, and the more they are foreseen, the greater the knowledge and intelligence we ascribe to the being by which it was ordained. In the earlier stages of our knowledge, we behold a multitude of distinct laws, all harmonising to produce results which we deem beneficial to our own species: as science advances, many of these minor laws are found to merge into some more general principles; and with its higher progress these secondary principles appear, in their turn, the mere consequences of some still more general law... All analogy leads us to infer, and new discoveries continually direct our expectation to the idea, that the most extensive laws to which we have hitherto attained, converge to some few simple and general principles, by which the whole of the material universe is sustained, and from which its infinitely varied phenomena emerge as the necessary consequences.

Charles Babbage Esq,
*The Ninth Bridgewater Treatise:
A Fragment*

Legally related phobias

Chrometophobia – fear of money (bad if you're a lawyer)

Decidophobia – fear of making decisions (bad if you're a judge)

Dikephobia – fear of justice

Eleutherophobia – fear of freedom (bad if you've just got out of jail)

Enosiophobia – fear of having committed an unpardonable sin

Harpaxophobia – fear of robbers

Hereiophobia – fear of challenges to official doctrine or of radical deviation (bad if you're thinking about committing a crime)

Kleptophobia – fear of stealing

Liticaphobia – fear of lawsuits

Mythophobia – fear of making false statements

Mastigophobia – fear of punishment

Peccatophobia – fear of sinning or imaginary crimes

Poinephobia – fear of punishment

Politicophobia – fear or abnormal dislike of politicians

Stygiophobia – fear of hell (particularly problematic if you're on Death Row)

Thantophobia – fear of dying (also bad on Death Row)

Uranophobia – fear of heaven (also bad on Death Row, especially if you're innocent)

QUOTE UNQUOTE

Some people think about sex all the time; some people think of sex some of the time; and some people never think about sex: they become lawyers.
Woody Allen, film director, writer and actor

WESTMINSTER HALL AND THE COURTS OF LAW

What is now Westminster Hall in London was once the Great Hall of the Royal Palace, where the King's Great Council met. It was out of this council that parliament and the courts of justice developed. By the end of the 1200s, the Courts of the Exchequer, Chancery, Common Pleas and the King's Bench were all based at Westminster, making it the centre of justice in England. Between 1820 and 1825 the architect Sir John Soane designed a number of buildings along the west side of the Hall that were used as the law courts. There they remained until they moved to the Royal Courts of Justice on the Strand in 1882. In its time, the Great Hall of the Royal Palace was the scene of some of the most sensational 'celebrity' trials in English history, including that of William Wallace (1305), Thomas More (1551), Guy Fawkes (1606) and Charles I (1649). All were sentenced to death.

Perhaps one of our most famous judges is a fictional one: 'Judge Dredd', as featured in the sci-fi comic *2000 AD*. This is his story:

When the Volgan War against the Eastern Bloc countries ended in 2023 AD, the population began to increase and there was a pressing need for new housing. Gradually a Mega-City arose around what was New York City and it was called Mega-City One. Construction was completed in 2034, by which time the population of America was approaching one billion. With a burgeoning population in such concentrated living conditions, a new kind of law enforcement was called for: the Judges. Dispensing with the need for reading rights and court appearances, the Judges were Justice with a capital J, authorised to administer the Law at their discretion and hand down sentences on the spot. Although Judges were initially the elite of the police force, they soon became an institution unto themselves, and it was not long before genetic control and cloning were used to produce Judges from a very young age. By 2047, when Mega-City Two and Mega-City Three had been built, there were no police any more and Judges alone were the law. The greatest of the Judges was Judge Dredd, whose favourite saying was, 'I am the law.'

As one of Mega-City One's most efficient and feared Judges, Judge Dredd met a number of arch-enemies in his time including: his clone-brother Rico Dredd whom he was forced to kill; the Judge Child whom Dredd decided was evil despite the prophesy he would save Mega-City One; Welch Logan who destroyed the World Trade Centre buildings in 2100 but who was interned on Devil's Island; the Angel Gang which included Mean Machine, who could set his head-butting dial on a scale from one to 10; the renegade droid Call-me-Kenneth who led a robot uprising; and the Dark Judges – Death, Fear, Fire and Mortis to mention but a few.

But of equal concern in the vast frying pan of humanity of Mega-City One were day-to-day infringements of the law. With unemployment running at nearly 90% by 2104, a number of illegal crazes swept the city, such as sky-surfing and heavyweight championship eating.

The lot of Judges in the Mega-Cities was not an easy one, so it was important that Judges were above the law and impervious to corruption or bribes. The penalty if they turned to the dark side? Rogue Judges were stripped of office, genetically modified to live in a vacuum, and banished to the penal colony of Titan to serve 20 years' hard labour.

When *2000 AD* magazine started in 1977, the creators perhaps did not imagine how popular Judge Dredd would become and that he might still be going strong into the third millennium. If they had, they might have changed the date on which the Judge Dredd story began: 1 January 1999.

---

54 *Percentage of adult males who reoffend within two years of leaving prison in Britain, according to 1997 statistics*

MOST CITED CASES IN US SUPREME COURT

Here are the 10 cases most often cited by the United States Supreme Court in its opinions between 1922 and 1999, and the number of times they were cited:

336 *Miranda v Arizona*, 384 US 436 (1966)
254 *New York Times Co v Sullivan*, 376 US 254 (1964)
248 *Cantwell v Connecticut*, 310 US 296 (1940)
241 *Erie Railroad Co v Tompkins*, 304 US 64 (1938)
240 *Boyd v United States*, 116 US 616 (1886)
220 *Gideon v Wainwright*, 372 US 335 (1963)
218 *McCulloch v Maryland*, 17 US 316 (1819)
211 *Mapp v Ohio*, 367 US 643 (1961)
209 *Brown v Board of Education of Topeka*, 347 US 483 (1954)
202 *Buckley v Valeo*, 424 US 1 (1976)

LITERATURE AND THE LAW

I know not whether Laws be right,
Or whether Laws be wrong;
All that we know who lie in gaol
Is that the wall is strong;
And that each day is like a year,
A year whose days are long.

But this I know, that every Law
That men have made for Man,
Since first Man took his brother's life,
And the sad world began,
But straws the wheat and saves the chaff
With a most evil fan.

This too I know – and wise it were
If each could know the same –
That every prison that men build
Is built with bricks of shame,
And bound with bars lest Christ should see
How men their brothers maim.

With bars they blur the gracious moon,
And blind the goodly sun:
And they do well to hide their Hell,
For in it things are done
That Son of God nor son of Man
Ever should look upon!

Oscar Wilde, *The Ballad of Reading Gaol*

Amount awarded, in hundreds of thousands of pounds, to Clint Eastwood in a 55
libel case over an accusation that he beat his wife

John Marshall

John Marshall (1755-1835) was the son of Thomas Marshall and Mary Randolph Keith. His parents decided that their son would be a lawyer and he didn't disappoint, although his private law practice flourished despite his penchant for slovenly dress. One of his clients, on seeing him in the street, exclaimed that he would never hire a man dressed like that to do even physical labour. But after hearing Marshall speak in court, the man changed his mind and begged him for representation.

Marshall became politically active and was appointed as Secretary of State in 1800 by President Adams, and then as Chief Justice of the US in 1801. Marshall was always concerned with preserving private property rights and the status and autonomy of the court. As the head of the US Supreme Court, he fathered the doctrine of judicial review with his decision in the case of *Marbury v Madison* in 1803. In it, he established that the Supreme Court had the power to declare acts of government (Congress) unconstitutional if they exceeded their powers. The effect was that the Supreme Court became in fact, as well as theory, an equal partner in government – a situation that remains today.

QUOTE UNQUOTE

I submit that an individual who breaks the law that conscience tells him is unjust and willingly accepts the penalty by staying in jail to arouse the conscience of the community over its injustice, is in reality expressing the very highest respect for law.
Martin Luther King Jr, US civil rights leader

PRIVATE PRISONS IN BRITAIN

To replace crumbling Victorian prisons and to cope with the ever increasing number of prisoners in Britain, the government has begun to turn to the private sector and give contracts for the operation of private prisons. Although most of Britain's 159 prisons are run by the Crown, the following are private:

Altcourse, *Liverpool*
Blakenhurst in Redditch, *Worcestershire*
Buckley Hall in Rochdale, *Lancashire*
Doncaster in Marshgate, *Doncaster*
Lowdham Grange in Lowdham, *Nottinghamshire*
Parc in Bridgend, *Wales*
The Wolds in Brough, *Yorkshire*

56 *Age of Iranian lawyer Shirin Ebadi when he was awarded the Nobel Peace prize in 2003*

LEGALLY MARRIED

Shoe Throwing

The marriage ceremony has given rise to some strange customs. In Europe and Asia, in addition to rice and food, which represented fertility, old shoes were often thrown at brides to wish them a healthy clutch of children. Shoes were considered to be a strong phallic symbol. Among the Inuit of the Arctic circle, a woman having difficulty conceiving carried around a piece of old shoe. The tradition continues today with shoes being tied to the back of a married couple's car, though tin cans have become more popular. Why? For the same reason that it was always old footwear – they are cheaper. However, if any new bride objects to being showered with shoes or rice, she should think herself lucky. In ancient Tibet, the local community would smear yak grease over newly-weds to ensure them good luck.

DEATH PENALTY FOR SEXUAL OFFENCES IN THE OLD TESTAMENT

The following sexual offences attracted the death penalty in the Old Testament:

1. Adultery and fornication *(Leviticus 20:10-12, Deuteronomy 22:22)*
2. Sex before marriage *(Deuteronomy 22:20-21)*
3. Sex when one person is engaged *(Deuteronomy 22:23-24)*
4. A priest's daughter practising prostitution *(Leviticus 21:9)*
5. Rape of someone who is engaged *(Deuteronomy 22:25)*
6. Having intercourse with animals *(Exodus 22:19)*
7. Incest *(Leviticus 20:11-12, 14, 19-21)*
8. Homosexuality *(Leviticus 20:13)*

Execution could be by burning, stoning, or using a spear, sword or arrow.

START THEM YOUNG

In October 2004, five-year old Nicolas White was playing at home in Bradley Stoke, Bristol when a man entered the house and grabbed a wallet off the kitchen table. 'Oi, what are you doing? That's not yours, put it back,' yelled Nicholas. The man fled, leaving behind a purse and a mobile phone, with Nicholas in hot pursuit. At the time, Nick's mum was in the garden and his dad was upstairs. 'My parents think I'm brave but I wasn't scared,' said Nicholas. His dad was proud, saying that Nick knew right from wrong and thought he was 'just really angry'. The burglar got away with £40.

Weeks taken to decide world's longest ever criminal trial in Hong Kong from November 1992 to November 1994 **57**

Pop musicians who have made albums about the law

Wayne Marshall – *Marshall Law*

Father MC – *Sex Is Law*

Lindsay Buckingham – *Law and Order*

Cheri – *Murphy's Law*

Facemob – *The Other Side of the Law*

Anne Clark – *The Law is an Anagram of Wealth*

Helloween – *Better Than Law*

Six Finger Satellite – *Law of Ruins*

Bill Neely – *Texas Law and Justice*

Catheters – *No Natural Law*

QUOTE UNQUOTE

The greatest single virtue of a strong legislature is not what it can do, but what it can prevent.
J William Fulbright, lawyer and politician

DEMOCRACY – NOT ALL THAT FAIR?

The system of democracy began centuries ago in Ancient Greece. Following a period of monarchies in the late Bronze Age (circa 2000-1200 BC), oligarchies in the Dark Age and tyrannies during the sixth century BC, the first democratic government was set up in Athens in 510 BC. The idea was that citizens would gather together in a public place and, following lively discussion, decide new laws. These days of course we can't all get together in one amphitheatre so we have elected representatives to do it for us. When that system fails us, as it sometimes seems to do, it is easy to idealise the early days of democracy when everyone had a say. However, it wasn't really as ideal as one might imagine. Athens at the time was a city ruling over an empire, which consisted of other Greek city-states. Citizens of these states had no say in decision-making whether they lived in their own city or were Metics (foreign traders and craftsmen) living in Athens itself. Citizens of Athens could be involved in the new democracy, but only men could be citizens, so women and children could not participate. In addition, there were a lot of slaves in Athens at the time who could not join in, although there was always the chance that they would be freed by their owners or buy their own freedom. Despite what might be perceived as a large degree of unfairness, democracy worked well and when Philip of Macedon conquered Greece, the democracy of Athens and other city-states was allowed to continue.

William Blackstone

Following an undistinguished career at the bar, William Blackstone (1723-80) turned to teaching, and on 25 October 1758 began his first lecture with an apology that he feared he would set back the law if his idea was 'crude or injudicious, or the execution of it lame or superficial'. However, his fears were unfounded. The series of lectures that he gave were published as *Commentaries on the Laws of England* between 1765 and 1769, and formed the backbone of the common law system in England for more than 100 years. They also had a profound effect on US law, influencing the Declaration of Independence, the US Constitution and US laws in general.

LEGAL QUANDARIES

A husband and a wife have consensual sexual intercourse. However, the husband has syphilis, a fact he's withheld from his wife, and she also contracts it. She wouldn't have consented if she'd known he was infected. Is the husband guilty of assault causing actual bodily harm?

Answer on page 153

DICK TURPIN: A LEGEND IN THE MAKING

Dick Turpin was born in 1706 in Essex and served an apprentice-ship as a butcher in Whitechapel, London, which was then on the outskirts of the city. After an early criminal career as a cattle rustler, he and a gang began to raid rural farmhouses and rob women of their valuables. By 1735 he was sufficiently notori-ous for the King to offer £50 for his capture. Turpin teamed up with a dandy, 'Captain' Tom King, and together they lived in a cave in Epping Forest and robbed passers-by. In 1737, when the price on his head had doubled to £100, Turpin shot dead a bounty hunter who had come to capture him. After a narrow escape, during which Turpin accidentally shot Tom King dead, he lived rough and for a while posed as a landed gentleman, occasionally riding off to steal horses and commit other crimes. He was eventually caught on a minor charge of shooting a cockerel, and identi-fied as the highwayman Dick Turpin and sentenced to death. His deeds were relatively seedy, but thanks to the 1834 novel *Rookwood* by Harrison Ainsworth, he was transformed into a legend. In his novel, Ainsworth attributed to Turpin a daring ride that was made on a black steed from Kent to York. The ride was actually made by highwayman John Nevison. However, Turpin – burglar, mur-derer and horse thief – was turned into a legend.

Before Stonewall (1984) – lesbian and gay retrospective balancing historical and political perspectives.

Behind the Rent Strike (1974) – examination of the 14-month rent strike in Kirby New Town, near Liverpool, 1973-74.

Dark Days (2000) – on the 'mole people' of Manhattan's abandoned train tunnels, where homeless people lived in underground communities.

Domestic Violence (2001) – a close look at wife-beating and other abuse, focusing on a shelter in Tampa, Florida.

Jung (War) – in the Land of the Mujaheddin (2000) – documentary about Northern Afghanistan fighting against the Russians and then the Taliban.

The Miners' Film (1975) – about the 1974 strike in Britain, a working-class film made by a collective of trade unionists.

The Thin Blue Line (1988) – investigation into the false imprisonment of Randall Adams for the shooting of a Dallas police officer in 1976.

Welfare (1975) – a harsh view of a New York Welfare Centre, and its strained social workers and clients.

Who Killed Vincent Chin? (1988) – compelling account of the murder of Chin, a Chinese American, and the attempt to bring his killers to justice.

LITERATURE AND THE LAW

[*There was*] a Society of Men among us, bred up from their Youth in the Art of proving by Words multiplied for the Pleasure, that White is Black, and Black is White, according as they are paid. To this Society all the rest of the People are as Slaves... In pleading, they studiously avoid entering into the Merits of the Cause; but are loud, violent, and tedious in dwelling upon all Circumstances which are not to the Purpose... It is likewise to be observed, that this Society has a peculiar Cant and Jargon of their own, that no other Mortal can understand, and wherein all their Laws are written, which they take special Care to multiply; whereby they have gone near to confound the very Essence of Truth and Falsehood, of Right and Wrong... In all Points out of their own Trade, they [*are*] usually the most Ignorant and stupid Generation among us, the most despicable in common Conversation, avowed Enemies to all Knowledge and Learning; and equally to pervert the general Reason of Mankind in every other Subject of Discourse, as in that of their own Profession.

Jonathan Swift, *Gulliver's Travels*, referring to lawyers

60 *Peak number of users, in millions, of Napster music-swapping internet service before it was shut down*

JUSTICE CLOTHES

*Godfrey had qualified as a lawyer years ago,
but no-one had yet seen him at the bar*

QUOTE UNQUOTE

*Justice is not to be taken by storm.
She is to be wooed by slow advances.*
Benjamin Cardozo, Associate Justice of the US Supreme Court

RELIGION AND THE LAW

Hinduism

Hinduism is the predominant religion in India. There are about 800 million Hindus in the world, and Hinduism is the third largest religion behind Christianity and Islam. It is characterised by a belief in karma, reincarnation and a caste system, a social system in which people are divided into four hierarchical groupings by birth. Hindus believe in a supreme being, Brahman, of many forms and natures. Deities such as Vishnu and Shiva are manifestations of this being. Opposing religions and beliefs are seen to be part of one eternal truth. Hindus desire to be free from earthly evils through the process of birth, life, death and rebirth, called *samsara*. A person can eventually escape *samsara* and achieve enlightenment.

HAVE YOU SEEN THIS MAN (OR WOMAN)?

The Federal Bureau of Investigation operates a programme called the FBI 10 most wanted fugitives. It dates from 1949 when a news story in the International News Service called for the FBI to release the names and details of the 10 'toughest guys' it wanted to capture. Such was the interest in the story that J Edgar Hoover, then director of the FBI, implemented a programme to do just that, which began in March 1950. The character of the list has changed over the decades, from consisting mainly of burglars, car thieves and bank robbers in the 1950s, to radicals who destroyed government property in the 1960s, to terrorists and organised criminals in the 1970s, where the focus remains today, along with serial killers and drug criminals.

There are two ways to get on the list:
1. You need a long record of committing serious offences and you need to be considered a dangerous menace to society in the light of present charges against you.
2. The FBI must think that you will 'benefit' from the publicity, in that you are not particularly notorious but will become so by being on the list and that this will help lead to your capture.

There are three ways to get off the list:
1. You are captured.
2. Charges against you are dropped.
3. You are no longer considered to be a particularly dangerous menace to society.

However, as there are only ever 10 people on the list, you can also lose your place if someone more dangerous comes along.

Of the 478 people who have been on the list, 449 have been found. Seven women have been on the list, the first of which was Ruth Eisemann-Schier in 1968.

WEIRD LAWS AROUND THE WORLD

Thailand
- You must not step on any currency in Thailand, as the image of the King is on all the money and it is seen as a disrespect toward him.
- You must pay a fine if you throw away used chewing gum on the street. If you don't pay, you can be jailed.
- Images of Buddha are sacred, so must be respected.
- When you're driving a car, you must wear a shirt.
- It's illegal to go out of your house if you're not wearing underwear.
- A man who forcibly subdues and has sexual intercourse with a female dog can only be charged with cruelty to animals. The fine is relatively small.

FICTION AND THE LAW

Fiction writers often take the law as their subject; here are a few who included it in the title:

Elmore Leonard – *The Law at Randado*
Lisa Scottoline – *Running from the Law*
Nancy Taylor Rosenberg – *Sullivan's Law*
Kristine Smith – *Law of Survival*
Christopher A Darden – *In Contempt*
T Lange – *Evidence Dismissed*
Chuck Logan – *The Big Law*
Wilkie Collins – *The Law and the Lady*
Laura Esquivel – *The Law of Love*
D Graham Burnett – *A Trial by Jury*

ALCOHOL AND THE LAW

The French wine, Fat Bastard, has been banned in Texas and Ohio, despite being distributed in 22 other states.

The Bureau of Alcohol, Tobacco and Firearms forbids the word 'refreshing' to be used to describe any alcoholic drink.

In Missouri, if you are under 21 and take out rubbish with even one empty alcohol bottle, you can be charged with illegal possession of alcohol.

In Iowa it is illegal to run up a tab in a bar, as set out by the Iowa Code.

Under the New Jersey Alcohol Beverage Control Law, it is illegal for parents to give their children under the age of 18 even one sip of alcohol.

Under the California Alcohol Beverage Control Act, no alcohol can be displayed within five feet of a cash register in any store in California that also sells fuel, just in case you get tempted.

In St Louis, Missouri it's illegal to sit on the side of the road and drink beer out of a bucket.

In Indiana it's illegal for a liquor store to sell cold soft drinks. However, it is permissible to sell warm soft drinks, under the Liquor Dealer Permits law.

In Fairbanks, Alaska it is illegal to give alcohol to a moose.

In the UK it's illegal to give alcohol to children under five. When you are 14 you can go into a pub or bar, but only if you drink soft drinks or low-alcohol beer. If you're 16 or 17 you can drink beer or cider with a meal, as long as you are accompanied by an adult. It's illegal to sell home brew but not to make it.

SOMETHING FISHY'S GOING ON

Do you keep fish in a pond? Or in a cold-water tank? If so, you need to be careful that your fish are legal, according to the Prohibition of Keeping or Release of Live Fish (Specified Species) Order 1998, pursuant to the Import of Live Fish (England and Wales) Act 1980. Some foreign fish are seen to be a threat to native species, and as such shop owners require a licence to sell them and fish keepers a licence to keep some of them. Fish caught by the Order include:

Blue Bream (*Abramis ballerus*)
Danubian bleak *(Chalcaburnus chalcoides)*
French nase *(Chrondrostoma toxostoma)*
Large-mouthed bass *(Micropterus salmoides)*
Snail-eating carp *(Mylopharyngodon piceus)*
Steelhead *(Oncorhynchus mykiss)*
Clicker barb or Topmouth gudgeon *(Pseudorasbora parva)*
Bitterling *(Rhodeus sericeus)*
Landlocked salmon *(Salmo salar)*
Zander *(Stizostedion)*
Vimba *(Vimba vimba)*

HE DEBITED FROM THE RICH
TO GIVE TO THE POOR

In October 2004 a man who stole from the rich to give to the poor was arrested in Wuerzburg, Bavaria. But this modern-day Robin Hood was no social outcast. Instead, he was a Wuerzburg bank manager. He was accused of moving almost £1 million from the accounts of wealthy customers into the accounts of customers with no money. About 70 cases were investigated. The 57 year-old bank manager, who was not named for legal reasons, said he didn't think that the rich would notice that their money was gone.

TAKE ME TO THE ALTAR

The countries with the highest rates of marriage in
2002, starting with the highest, are:

1. Antigua and Barbuda
2. Maldives
3. Barbados
4. Liechtenstein
5. Cyprus
6= Seychelles and South Africa
8. Jamaica
9= Ethiopia and Iran

64 *Maximum speed, in kilometres an hour, of the world's smallest street-legal car, the Peel P50*

THE 10 COMMANDMENTS

The 10 Commandments as given to Moses by God form the basis of Christian morality and many Western laws. According to the Old Testament, God summoned Moses to the top of Mount Sinai in order to pass on his Commandments carved on two stone tablets. Exodus 20 states that the 10 Commandments are:

1. I am the Lord your God, who brought you out of the land of Egypt, out of the house of bondage. You shall have no other gods before me.
2. You shall not make for yourself a graven image. You shall not bow down to them or serve them.
3. You shall not take the name of the Lord your God in vain.
4. Remember the Sabbath day, to keep it holy.
5. Honour your father and your mother.
6. You shall not kill.
7. You shall not commit adultery.
8. You shall not steal.
9. You shall not bear false witness against your neighbour.
10. You shall not covet your neighbour's house, wife, manservant, maidservant, his ox, his ass, or anything of his.

However, when Moses descended from Mount Sinai he found his people had created a molten calf and were singing and dancing around it. Moses was so angry that he smashed the stone tablets on which the Commandments were written and destroyed the calf. On God's command Moses made new stone tablets, climbed Mount Sinai and was given the Commandments again. However, this time they were different. Exodus 34 states that the 10 Commandments are:

1. Thou shalt worship no other god for the Lord is a jealous god.
2. Thou shalt make thee no molten gods.
3. The feast of unleavened bread shalt thou keep in the month when the ear is on the corn.
4. All the first-born are mine.
5. Six days shalt thou work, but on the seventh thou shalt rest.
6. Thou shalt observe the feast of weeks, even of the first fruits of the wheat harvest, and the feast of ingathering at the year's end.
7. Thou shalt not offer the blood of my sacrifice with leavened bread.
8. The fat of my feast shall not remain all night until the morning.
9. The first of the first fruits of thy ground thou shalt bring unto the house of the Lord thy God.
10. Thou shalt not seethe a kid in its mother's milk.

To this day, barristers wear a double-tabbed linen band that is used as a collar. The tabs represent the two tablets on which Moses was given the 10 Commandments.

TRUTH OR FICTION

According to a 2000 survey of around 300 films made between 1930 and 1970 in which lawyers had major parts, in over 66% of those films the lawyer was portrayed in a positive light – as an able, moral professional doing their job well. However, since 1970 the trend has been reversed and in over two-thirds of the films surveyed, lawyers were portrayed as either bad people or negligent, immoral professionals. More worryingly for dismayed lawyers everywhere, there is a theory, known as the cultivation effect, which suggests that the public may be learning their attitude towards lawyers from films, rather than films reflecting the truth.

FAMOUS PEOPLE WITH LAW NAMES

Jude Law, *actor*
Courtney Cox, *actress*
Nigel Lawson, *former Chancellor of the Exchequer*
Denis Law, *Scottish footballer*
Emma Chambers, *actress*
Nigella Lawson, *cook and TV presenter*
Sue Lawley, *broadcaster*
Judge Dread, *musician*
Kate Lawlor, *Big Brother reality TV show winner*
Courtney Love, *musician*

LITERATURE AND THE LAW

Charles Darwin ponders the laws of natural selection

We can, in short, see why nature is prodigal in variety, though niggard in innovation. But why this should be a law of nature if each species has been independently created no man can explain.

Many other facts are, as it seems to me, explicable on this theory. How strange it is that a bird, under the form of a woodpecker, should prey on insects on the ground; that upland geese, which rarely or never swim, would possess webbed feet; that a thrush-like bird should dive and feed on sub-aquatic insects; and that a petrel should have the habits and structure fitting it for the life of an auk! and so in endless other cases. But on the view of each species constantly trying to increase in number, with natural selection always ready to adapt the slowly varying descendants of each to any unoccupied or ill-occupied place in nature, these facts cease to be strange, or might even have been anticipated.

Charles Darwin, *The Origin of Species*

IGNORANCE OF THE LAW IS NO DEFENCE

When travelling it's important, if not to actually blend in with the locals, to at least not break the law by what you do or don't wear. Here are some laws that will help you to stay on the straight and narrow.

If you are in Tucson, Arizona and you are a woman you may not wear trousers. But if you are in Miami and you are a man, you can't wear a strapless gown.

Surprisingly, in Hawaii you can't go out in public wearing only your swimming costume. However, if you are in Kentucky and you are a woman you can wear a swimming costume on a highway if, and only if, you are accompanied by two policeman or you are armed with a club or you are lighter than 90 pounds or heavier than 200 pounds. Makes sense really.

It's against the law to fish in pyjamas in Chicago.

And it's not just people. In Georgia it's illegal to change the clothes of a mannequin in the front window without first pulling the curtains.

Finally, it may not be just what you are wearing. In Chicago, if you are are diseased, mutilated or deformed to the extent that you yourself are an unsightly or disgusting object, you can't go out in public at all. So there, Quasimodo.

QUOTE UNQUOTE

When the president does it, that means it is not illegal.
Richard Nixon, US President, in May 1977, three years after he resigned over the Watergate scandal before impeachment proceedings could begin against him

MONKEY BUSINESS

When Austrian police started getting complaints in October 2004 about a gorilla that was terrorising elderly walkers in the hills near the towns of St Margarethen, Rust and Oggau, they initially assumed it was a hoax. The idea of a gorilla jumping out of the bushes at terrified elderly folk and then running away seemed unlikely. However, after receiving dozens of complaints, they decided to take it seriously and set up a special hunting team of marksmen with tranquilliser guns and tracker dogs. It wasn't long before they caught the 'gorilla' – a 25-year-old man wearing a gorilla suit. He didn't need to be sedated. Instead he apologised and said that the place was so boring he'd decided to give people something to talk about. He was released on bail, but only after he agreed to hand in his furry suit.

Some of the great music of Western society has come out of the US. The freedom of expression in music we generally take for granted today is the result of a hard-fought battle between musicians and the law in the States.

The conflict began in earnest in the 1950s, when the major reason to censor music was sexual suggestiveness in song lyrics. Violence was also occasionally cited; Link Wray's instrumental 'Rumble' was dropped from playlists in 1959 because the title alone was said to provoke teenage violence.

In the 1950s jukeboxes were an important source of music for the public. Police in California, Long Beach and Memphis confiscated jukeboxes in 1954 for stocking illicit music, and there were bans on jukeboxes across the country. Apart from taking the jukeboxes away and banning suggestive songs, the other way to deal with the menace of popular music was to change the lyrics of songs. For example, Cole Porter's 'I get no kick from cocaine', arguably not an incitement to take drugs at all, was changed to 'I get perfume from Spain'.

The 1960s saw a similar fear of suggestiveness in lyrics, and of anti-war sentiment, as The Doors' 'Unknown Soldier' was banned. The FBI kept an eye on certain musicians, including Bob Dylan, Woody Guthrie and Jim Morrison. The Rolling Stones'

'I Can't Get No Satisfaction' was banned across America in 1965 for its risqué lyrics. Some radio stations banned it because the line 'Baby come back next week, cause you see I'm on a losing streak', was somewhat imaginatively interpreted as being about menstruation. But it was not just the authorities who kicked up a fuss. In 1966, members of the public burned Beatles' records in response to John Lennon's claims that the Beatles' popularity matched that of Jesus Christ. It is said that at one point John Lennon believed himself to be Jesus Christ, perhaps a victim of his own power of suggestion, and certainly a source of worry for some of his friends and his record label. In 1969 the New York police confiscated 30,000 copies of John and Yoko's album, *Two Virgins*, because it featured a picture of the couple naked on the cover.

The 1970s saw the emphasis shift to concern about drugs. Peter, Paul and Mary's song 'Puff the Magic Dragon' was criticised by the Illinois Crime Commission for drug references, an accusation Peter, Paul and Mary denied. An innocent casualty was John Denver's 'Rocky Mountain High', for fear it referred to a drug high. And the sexual concerns continued – in 1975 the Reverend Charles Boykin of Florida came up with the startling statistic that of the 1,000 unmarried mothers that he interviewed, 984 fell pregnant under the influence of rock music. In Britain too music faced a battle with censorship. The Sex Pistols' 'God Save the Queen', released in the Queen's Silver Jubilee year of 1977, was banned by the BBC.

By the 1980s the territory was well-trodden, with one noteworthy development being the parental warning sticker on CDs. This resulted from Senator Al Gore's wife, Tipper, hearing explicit lyrics on the song 'Little Nikki' on Prince's *Purple Rain* album. She organised a pressure group and by 1990 the music industry began voluntarily putting 'Tipper stickers' on records. Back in the 1980s, the issue of teenage suicide emerged, and MTV banned the Replacements' song 'The Ledge' for fear it encouraged teenagers to kill themselves. In Britain, 'Relax' by Frankie Goes to Hollywood, with its suggestive lyrics, was banned from Radio 1, famously being cut-off mid-song when the DJ heard the lyrics. The issue of music's effects on teens became more prominent in the 1990s and into the new millennium, and Marilyn Manson's music was accused of inspiring Eric Harris and Dylan Klebold, the perpetrators of the Columbine High School massacre.

However, despite ongoing friction with the law, freedom of musical expression has come a long way since police officers threatened to arrest Elvis Presley for obscenity if he moved at all during his performances in San Diego in 1955, after his swivelling hips raised eyebrows and moral concerns all over the world.

Other songs that have been banned over the years include: 'Physical' by Olivia Newton-John ; 'George Jackson' by Bob Dylan; 'Ohio' by Neil Young; 'Pictures of Lily' by The Who; 'Original Sin' by INXS; 'Spasticus Autisticus' by Ian Dury; 'Truly Yours' by Kool G Rap and D J Polo; 'I Bet You They Won't Play This Song on the Radio' by Monty Python (demonstrating precognition); and 'Wham Bam, Thank You Ma'am' by Dean Martin.

PRIME-TIME LAW

Some of the most successful prime-time TV shows about lawyers
The Law and Mr Jones (1960-62)
The Defenders (1961-65)
Judd, For the Defence (1967-69)
LA Law (1986-1994)
Equal Justice (1990-91)
Law & Order (1990-)
The Practice (1997-)
Family Law (1999-)

LEGAL TEASERS

Command the Italian car (4 letters)
Answer on page 153

LITERATURE AND THE LAW

Stranger to civil and religious rage,
The good man walked innoxious through his age.
No courts he saw, no suits would ever try,
Nor dared an oath, nor hazarded a lie:
Unlearned, he knew no schoolman's subtle art,
No language, but the language of the heart.
By nature honest, by experience wise,
Healthy by temp'rance and by exercise,
His life, though long, to sickness passed unknown,
His death was instant, and without a groan.
O grant me thus to live, and thus to die!
Alexander Pope, *An Epistle from Mr Pope to Dr Arbuthnot*

QUOTE UNQUOTE

*Only lawyers and mental defectives are
automatically exempt for jury service.*
George Bernard Shaw, Irish dramatist and writer

RELIGION AND THE LAW

Shinto

Shinto is a Japanese religion that began about 500 BC, although it is really a combination of all the belief systems of ancient Japan and has no founder, text, God or moral laws. According to Shinto, there is no split between the physical world and a supernatural one. Shinto is widespread throughout Japan and in this sense is a national religion. It is very much concerned with an individual's day-to-day life, and so it is less a religion and more a way of life. The majority of Japanese practise both Shinto and Buddhism. The word 'Shinto' derives from the Chinese 'shin tao' or 'path of the gods'. Shinto believes in 'kami', or gods, but they are unlike gods of other religions. They are many things, including deities related to animals and objects in nature, protective deities and natural phenomena like earthquakes. They also include special people (until the end of World War II the Emperor was believed to be divine). They are very similar to people and are usually considered to be benevolent. Shinto is concerned primarily with ritual and there are thousands of shrines of greatly varying size throughout Japan, where both kami and ancestors are worshipped.

70 *Years after an author's death at which copyright expires*

Reginald's cunning plan to trip up on purpose, then sue the council for damages, unfortunately went a tad too far.

A FULL HOUSE

Fancy a friendly hand of poker? Watch out if you're in the US, because it's illegal in 20 states to play a friendly game for money, even for token amounts. And in 30 other states you can be arrested and taken away for 'aggravated gambling'. The definition of 'aggravated gambling' varies from state to state, but generally means high-stakes or professional gambling in the home, and usually applies to repeat offences. Early in 2004, seven friends fell foul of these laws in a cabin in Chickasaw State Park near Jackson, Tennessee. Despite the fact that one of their number was the Chickasaw State Park's manager, and another was a retired cop, the cabin was stormed by police and $20 was confiscated. 'We were cooking a stew and relaxing,' said the park manager. 'It wasn't a big deal.' However, the Chester County Court thought very differently, and they were each fined $50. In other states the penalties can be higher – anything from misdemeanour fines to felony convictions and even prison sentences. Prison would usually only be for repeat offending of high-stakes poker, although you can still be arrested for that in your own home.

FAMOUS PEOPLE WHO USED TO BE LAWYERS

Clive Anderson (1952-), *TV comedian*
Clement Attlee (1883-1967), *Prime Minister*
Alfred Austin (1835-1913), *Poet Laureate*
John Buchan (1875-1940), *statesman, historian, and writer*
Clarissa Dickson Wright (1947-), *cook, writer and broadcaster*
Vassily Kandinsky (1866-1944), *Russian expressionist painter*
Vladimir Lenin (1870-1924),
Marxist theoretician, First Premier of the Soviet Union
Nelson Mandela (1918-),
black South African statesman, President of South Africa
Jawaharlal Nehru (1889-1964),
first Prime Minister of independent India
Charles Reade (1814-84), *novelist*
Sir Walter Scott (1771-1832), *novelist and poet*
Jerry Springer, *US television presenter*
Noah Webster (1758-1843), *US lexicographer*
Yohji Yamamoto (1943-), *fashion designer*

LAWYERS WHO FELL FOUL OF THE LAW

After graduating from New York Law School, Julius Richard 'Dixie' Davis worked for two law firms before setting up his own practice in Manhattan. He began his foray into illegality in a small way, as a pliable lawyer for clients running numbers rackets (numbers was an illegal gambling game, also called bolito, that was very popular in Harlem). Through his shady connections, he became involved with 'Dutch Shultz' who by 1930 ruled New York in a similar way to which Al Capone ruled Chicago, although Schultz was said to be much nastier than Capone. Davis realised he was in deep when Schultz murdered a man named Jules Martin right in front of him. Davis recounted the moment some four years later: 'It is very unhealthy to be an eyewitness to a murder when a man like Schultz is the killer. To a man like him the only good witness is a dead witness. As I ran, I kept thinking of the mess I was in and I couldn't help longing for the days when I was just a Kid Mouthpiece, making lots of money as a shyster in the magistrate's court.' Nevertheless, Davis helped smooth things over and Schultz came to trust and depend on him. When Schultz was killed by rival gangsters, Davis found himself less protected and in 1938 was indicted for his part in a numbers racket conspiracy. In 1939 he went to prison but only served a year. He then moved west to start a new life and, as far as we know, never troubled the authorities again.

Some of the most notorious criminal families

Bonanno family – started by Joe Bonanno in 1930s New York; his successors were Natale Evola and Phil Rastelli.

Chicago family – run by Al Capone until his imprisonment in 1931, when Paul Ricca took over until 1972.

Cleveland family – run by James 'Blackie' Licavoli; he had members of the FBI in his pocket.

Gambino family – one of the most famous New York crime families, named after Carlo Gambino in the 1950s. John Gotti was its head before his incarceration in 1992. Gotti died in 2002.

Genovese family – another New York crime family, run by Vito Genovese; inconveniently, he had to run it from a jail cell for some time.

Luchese family – started by Joe Masseria in 1953; taken over by Tommy Luchese. The gang was involved in controlling the New York garment industry.

Luciano family – New York outfit run by Charles 'Lucky' Luciano until, in a not-so-lucky turn of events, Vito Genovese took over; however, shortly afterwards he went to prison.

Mangano family – run by Vincent Mangano whose speciality was New York waterfront rackets.

Morello family – run by brothers from Corleone, Italy in the late 1800s.

Pillow Gang – from St Louis; their head, Carmelo Fresina, was shot in the buttocks and thereafter needed a pillow to sit on.

Purple Gang – predominantly Jewish family from Detroit, renowned for its violent tactics during Prohibition.

LITIGATION, ANYONE?

Japan has one lawyer per 10,000 citizens. The US has one lawyer per 390 citizens. In the US, for every 1,000 trained lawyers there are 100 trained engineers – in Japan it is the other way around. However, all that is beginning to change. In April 2004, Japan brought a law into force that permits foreign lawyers to practise law in Japan for the first time since 1955. The first to take advantage of this were three US attorneys. Since then, other foreign lawyers have also applied to open practices in Japan. Japan is not currently a litigious society, but as many an economist has observed, supply can sometimes create demand. Watch this space.

Number of lawyers McDonalds employ in the US (with a further 60 in 19 other countries) to defend lawsuits **73**

LEGAL PERSONALITIES

Sir John Vaughan

Sir John Vaughan (1603-74) was a Lord Chief Justice whose main legacy is his decision in Bushell's Case. In that case, charges were brought against two men, William Penn and William Mead. In Sir John's words, the men appeared before the court 'for certain trespasses, contempts, unlawful assemblies and tumults, made and perpetrated by the said Penn and Mead, together with divers other unknown persons, to the number of 300, unlawfully and tumultuously assembled in Grace-Church-street in London, to the disturbance of the peace, whereof the said Penn and Mead were then indicted before the said justices. Upon which indictment, the said Penn and Mead pleaded they were Not Guilty.' Edward Bushell, a juryman, gave a not guilty verdict. As a result he was imprisoned. Sir John Vaughan, in a 13,000-word judgment, held that a jury is right to act on its judgment and should not be punished for coming to a decision that the Crown disagrees with. Previous to this decision, if a jury found someone not guilty and the King didn't agree with their decision, he simply had the jury imprisoned instead.

QUOTE UNQUOTE

May you have a lawsuit in which you know you are in the right.
Gypsy proverb.

FOR WHOM THE BAR TOLLS

Ernest Hemingway, the hard-drinking novelist, recently became the cause of a dispute between two bars in his home town of Key West, Florida. The first, Sloppy Joe's Bar, was located in a disused morgue from 1933 and was named after one of Hemingway's drinking buddies. However, the bar moved half a block away in 1937, taking the Sloppy Joe name with it, and the old morgue became Captain Tony's Saloon, although it continued to claim that it was the original Sloppy Joe's. To back up this claim, the bar displayed a photograph of Hemingway fishing, one of his passions when not drinking, with the original owner, Captain Tony Tarracino. In July 2004 the owners of Sloppy Joe's Bar tried to get a US district judge to stop Captain Tony's Saloon making the claim. At the time of going to press, the result was still pending. However, perhaps the dispute would be better resolved by the local Monroe County historian Tom Hambright who, when asked which bar Hemingway drank in, replied, 'Both, as far as I can determine.'

74 *Age of the oldest inmate to be put to death in the US since 1941*

I SENTENCE YOU TO 50 PRESS-UPS

When two teenage boys appeared in court in Kentucky in 2003 charged with driving at 20 miles per hour over the speed limit, they were expecting to have their licenses suspended. However, they hadn't figured on appearing before District Judge Dan Ballot, who had spent seven years in the US Marines. So, in addition to having to attend traffic school and write a five-page essay on what they'd learns there, the teenagers were required to do press-ups in court. The judge didn't specify how many, although one of the boys was sufficiently enthusiastic to do, in his opinion, 40 or 50. Judge Ballot, whose unorthodox methods might be explained by the fact that he had only just begun working as a judge, said, 'They just needed to have their eyes opened a little bit. I just wanted to make them squirm a bit.'

AMERICA'S TOP 10 LAW SCHOOLS

According to the US News & World Report's Annual Law School Ranking for 2005, the top 10 US law schools are:

1. Yale University
2. Harvard University
3. Stanford University
4. Columbia University
5. New York University
6. University of Chicago
7. University of Michigan-Ann Arbor
8. University of Pennsylvania
9. University of Virginia
10. Duke University

LITERATURE AND THE LAW

These wonderful narrations inspired me with strange feelings. Was man, indeed, at once so powerful, so virtuous and magnificent, yet so vicious and base? He appeared at one time a mere scion of the evil principle, and at another as all that can be conceived of noble and godlike. To be a great and virtuous man appeared the highest honour that can befall a sensitive being; to be base and vicious, as many on record have been, appeared the lowest degradation, a condition more abject than that of the blind mole or harmless worm. For a long time I could not conceive how one man could go forth to murder his fellow, or even why there were laws and governments; but when I heard details of vice and bloodshed, my wonder ceased, and I turned away with disgust and loathing.

Mary Shelley, *Frankenstein*

Percentage of robberies in the UK that are committed in the 88 most deprived 75
local authorities

'Hmm. Says here the law is a Mr Bumble...'

LEGAL TEASERS

Question: What do you call a friendly, polite, sober person at a
convention of barristers and solicitors?
Answer on page 153

CRIMINAL OFFENCES AND OMISSION

The following offences can be committed, in the eyes of the law, by
omitting to do something, rather than performing an action:

Murder.
Manslaughter.
Unlawful detention.
Causing serious injury with intent.
Abduction.
Aggravated abduction.
Kidnapping.

For example, you can cause unlawful detention by omitting to
unlock a door; you can cause serious injury with intent by failing
to turn off machinery that a factory colleague has got caught in;
and a doctor could commit murder by omitting to give necessary
treatment. A crime by omission will often be where you owe a duty
of care to another person.

76 *Year in the eighteenth century when Thomas Jefferson wrote the Declaration of Independence*

HIT THE ROAD, JACK, AND
DON'T YOU COME BACK

According to Interpol, the countries with the highest reported
number of car thefts in 2002, per 100,000 population,
in descending order are:

1. Switzerland
2. New Zealand
3. England and Wales
4. Sweden
5. Australia
6. Denmark
7. Scotland
8. Italy
9. Canada
10. Norway

BAD LAWYERS OR GOOD

Walter Bagehot (1826-77), an economist and journalist, was perhaps the greatest commentator on parliament and the monarchy in Victorian England. After being a banker, he was editor of *The Economist* from 1860 until his death. His numerous writings included a definitive text on the English Constitution and an essay written in 1876 called 'Bad Lawyers or Good', in which he muses on the unintelligibility of the law and argues for its simplification:

'It may be said that it would be quite useless for clients commonly to see counsel, for the points which counsel have to decide on are so technical that the client cannot understand them. But ought they to be so technical? Ought not the main gist of all cases to be intelligible to men of business interested in them, and anxious to attend to them? In matter of fact, I believe that almost all the law of moneyed property is now intelligible to careful men of that sort; and if the law of landed property is not intelligible, it is only because that law is bad. Mysteries in practical affairs are very dangerous; the more so because, when they once exist, many quiet, unimaginative people cannot help saying and believing that they are inevitable and necessary. But any one who rouses his mind to ask in a specific case, "How does this law come to be so unintelligible?" will find that the reasons for it belong to some bygone time, and that now it wants to be altered and fitted to modern life. Nothing will ever simplify law so much as the making lawyers explain it to non-lawyers.'

MURDER MOST HORRIBLE

According to Interpol, the countries with the highest reported number of murders in 2000, per 100,000 people, in descending order are:

1. Honduras
2. South Africa
3. Swaziland
4. Colombia
5. Lesotho
6. Rwanda
7. Jamaica
8. El Salvador
9. Venezuela
10. Bolivia

QUOTE UNQUOTE

My fellow Americans, I am pleased to tell you I just signed legislation which outlaws Russia for ever. The bombing begins in five minutes.
Ronald Reagan, US President, on a radio test in 1984, unaware that he could be heard

LEGALLY MARRIED

Tribes of the Philippines

Filipino people in Luzon, like the Tagalogs, Ilocanos and Pangasinenses, practise the custom of pinning money onto the clothes of the bride and groom while they dance. The bride and groom's family have a competition to see who can pin the most money on either the bride or the groom. At the end they add it up, applaud the winning family, but then give the money to the married couple.

The Aetas of Zambales eat from the same plate while they get married, taking turns to feed each other. A man may also take more than one wife, but only if he has enough 'bandi', a form of dowry, which can be anything from bows and arrows or large knives (bolos) to money.

The mountain people of the Igorot, on the other hand, have a trial marriage, or 'dap-ay', where boys live and sleep with girls their own age. The girls live in a room called an 'egban' and are visited at night by the boys. When a couple become attached, they live together until the girl becomes pregnant. Then, once gifts are given, chickens sacrificed and omens read, the wedding can take place. In the actual ceremony they eat rice together and drink from the same cup.

Study of the law is divided up into a number of major subject areas. Although university courses vary, a typical selection facing a student who has passed their first year's study will consist of some of the following subjects:

TORTS – a tort is an injury or a wrong. Torts may be committed with force, as trespasses, which can be an injury to a person, like assault, battery or imprisonment, or to property. Torts may also be committed without force, which would include an injury to the rights of persons, or to personal property, or to real property.

CONTRACT LAW – is the branch of jurisprudence that studies the rights and obligations of parties entering into contracts. A contract is a binding legal agreement between two or more persons in law. Contract law covers all aspects of a contract, whether it is a business contract or a marriage contract.

EQUITY LAW – is a branch of the legal system in the English common law tradition that resolves disputes between persons by using principles of fairness and justice. Equity often comes into play when none of the parties to a dispute has done anything against the law, but their rights or claims are in conflict. Thus, it is to be contrasted with 'law' proper, which is composed of statute or common law.

JURISPRUDENCE – can mean two different things. In the context of the common law, it means case law; that is, the law decided by the courts and other officials. Its second meaning is the philosophy of law or legal theory. It is the study not of particular laws in specific countries but of the attributes of law in general in societies.

CRIMINAL LAW – concerns the principles of criminal liability, including the procedure on indictment and summary procedure. Selected offences may be examined with reference to case law.

PUBLIC LAW – examines the ideas and workings of a constitution, government institutions, the exercise of public power and relations between the state and citizens. This leads to examining controls on the use of public power, and the process of judicial review.

LAND LAW – gives a history and the principles of land law, including how the concepts of private and public land came into being.

COMMERCIAL LAW – is about the law regarding the sale and transfer of goods including hire purchase and bailment, negotiable instruments, and charges upon and securities over personal property, including guarantees and applicable aspects of agency, insurance and insolvency.

DOMINATRIX BARBIE WINS THE DAY

Mattel Inc, makers of the Barbie doll – the smiling, clean-haired, clean-living toy beloved of little girls everywhere – took exception to a British doll maker who transformed Barbie into the risqué, partly nude Dungeon Doll. This Barbie wasn't one for tea and cake in the kitchen; she wore a rubber bondage outfit and helmet and was ready to discipline the naughty. Yet despite using what looked like Barbie in the Dungeon Doll, the court held that the copyrights of Mattel Inc were not infringed. The judge observed that the Dungeon Doll was 'quite different' to Mattel's other products for children and was no threat to sales of Barbie dolls. It's unclear whether Ken has decided to dump Barbie yet for her naughtier rival.

LITERATURE AND THE LAW

A fox may steal your hens, sir,
A whore your health and pence, sir,
Your daughter rob your chest, sir,
Your wife my steal your rest, sir,
A thief your goods and plate.
But this is all but picking,
With rest, pence, chest and chicken;
It ever was decreed, sir,
If lawyer's hand is fee'd, sir,
He steals your whole estate.

John Gay, *The Beggar's Opera*

FAMOUS LAWYERS

John Mortimer

Born in 1923, John Mortimer is a novelist, playwright and TV dramatist. His work includes a trilogy of political novels (*Paradise Postponed*, *Titmuss Regained*, and *The Sound of Trumpets*), and numerous successful plays and television shows. His body of work includes over 50 books, scripts and plays. His creation Rumpole of the Bailey, who first appeared in Mortimer's *Play for Today* in 1975, is beloved by fans not only in Britain but around the world. Rumpole is extremely successful in the US. In fact, reference was made to the show twice during the OJ Simpson trial, with a defence attorney stating, 'As Mrs Rumpole would put it, I think we have a case of premature adjudication'. Although he is best known for his writing, Mortimer was called to the bar in 1948 – and it was his career as a barrister that provided inspiration for many of his stories.

FILMS IT IS ILLEGAL TO WATCH

Film censors are constantly assessing the suitability of films for public viewing and giving ratings, from 'Universal for All' to 'R18'. However, some films are considered to be beyond the pale and are banned. Here are a few of them:

Savage Temptation – banned in 40 countries.

Cannibal Ferox – banned in 31 countries.

Snuff – banned 20 years ago.

The Last House on the Left – banned 30 years ago and still banned in the UK and New Zealand.

Baise-Moi – still banned in the UK, Australia and New Zealand.

Salo – first banned in 1976.

I Spit on Your Grave – banned in most Asian countries.

The House on the Edge of the Park – banned in 32 countries.

A Clockwork Orange – banned in numerous countries and still banned in Ireland, Singapore and South Korea. Curiously, *A Clockwork Orange* was voluntarily banned in Britain for 30 years by the director, Stanley Kubrick, following strong reaction to the film on its initial release in 1972. The ban expired with Kubrick's death in 1999.

ROCK AND ROLL JUSTICE

One of the more unusual arrests of a celebrity occurred in December 1967. The Doors, fronted by the legendary singer Jim Morrison, performed a concert in New Haven. Before the show began, Jim Morrison was discovered by a policeman in a compromising position with a young woman in a shower stall near his dressing room backstage. Not realising Jim was the star of the show, the policeman ordered him to leave. He refused, telling the officer in no uncertain terms to 'eat it'. The officer sprayed mace in Morrison's face before his identity was revealed. The singer recovered, took to the stage and the concert began. Some way into The Doors' set the show was interrupted. The police claimed they came on stage because Morrison was giving an indecent performance. Others at the concert claimed that he was simply telling the story about how the officer had sprayed mace in his face and the police didn't like it. Whichever interpretation is true, the lights were turned on, Jim Morrison was arrested onstage, and everyone was told to go home. That's rock and roll for you.

The narrator has killed an old man and disposed of the body under the floorboards. When the police arrive, he is confident of escaping the law and encourages them to search the house. He is so confident of his 'perfect triumph' that he invites the officers to sit down, and places his own chair over where the body lies...

The officers were satisfied. My MANNER had convinced them. I was singularly at ease. They sat and while I answered cheerily, they chatted of familiar things. But, ere long, I felt myself getting pale and wished them gone. My head ached, and I fancied a ringing in my ears; but still they sat, and still chatted. The ringing became more distinct: I talked more freely to get rid of the feeling: but it continued and gained definitiveness – until, at length, I found that the noise was NOT within my ears.

No doubt I now grew VERY pale; but I talked more fluently, and with a heightened voice. Yet the sound increased – and what could I do? It was A LOW, DULL, QUICK SOUND – MUCH SUCH A SOUND AS A WATCH MAKES WHEN ENVELOPED IN COTTON. I gasped for breath, and yet the officers heard it not. I talked more quickly, more vehemently but the noise steadily increased.

I arose and argued about trifles, in a high key and with violent gesticulations; but the noise steadily increased. Why WOULD they not be gone? I paced the floor to and fro with heavy strides, as if excited to fury by the observations of the men, but the noise steadily increased. O God! what COULD I do? I foamed – I raved – I swore! I swung the chair upon which I had been sitting, and grated it upon the boards, but the noise arose over all and continually increased. It grew louder – louder – louder! And still the men chatted pleasantly, and smiled. Was it possible they heard not? Almighty God! – no, no? They heard! – they suspected! – they KNEW! – they were making a mockery of my horror! – this I thought, and this I think. But anything was better than this agony! Anything was more tolerable than this derision! I could bear those hypocritical smiles no longer! I felt that I must scream or die! – and now – again – hark! louder! louder! louder! LOUDER!

'Villains!' I shrieked, 'dissemble no more! I admit the deed! – tear up the planks! – here, here! – it is the beating of his hideous heart!'

Edgar Allan Poe,
The Tell-Tale Heart

QUOTE UNQUOTE

No law or ordinance is mightier than understanding.
Plato, Athenian philosopher

---

82 *Age of Florence Allen, appointed in 1920 as first woman judge of the US court of common pleas, when she died in 1966*

A FRAGRANT WIFE

Shortly after Margaret Thatcher appointed Jeffrey Archer her deputy party leader in 1985, his political career seemed to be in ruins when the *Daily Star* newspaper claimed that he had paid a prostitute for her services and subsequently for her silence. He resigned, but sued the *Daily Star* for libel in 1987. The judge's infamous finding in Archer's favour seemed to be heavily influenced by the smell of his wife, Mary. The judge suggested that Archer had no need of cold, rubber-insulated sex in a seedy hotel because of the allure of his wife. The judge asked: 'Has she elegance? Is she not fragrant?' Archer won the case and the *Daily Star* had to pay £500,000 damages. However, years later a friend who had testified on Archer's behalf at the trial admitted he had lied about Archer's whereabouts. Archer was subsequently convicted of perjury and perverting the course of justice and in 2001, to the ill-disguised glee of his original accusers, he was sentenced to four years in prison.

REALITY COURT TV

Reality television shows about courts – some of which have real judges and lawyers – include:

Curtis Court • *Divorce Court*
Judge Mathis • *Judge Mills Lane* • *Judge Joe Brown*
Judge Judy • *Judge Wapner* • *Moral Court*
Morning Court • *Night Court* • *The People's Court*
Small Claims Court • *Texas Justice*
They Stand Accused • *Traffic Court*

LEGAL PERSONALITIES

Karl Christian Friedrich Krause

Karl Christian Friedrich Krause (1781-1832) was a German philosopher. His views on the nature of God were influential, particularly in Spain where his followers were called *krausistas*. Krause developed the concept of pantheism, in which God is a reality of which man, nature and the universe are manifestations. Krause's work deeply influenced modern law, in that he took a philosophical view of law rather than using only the ideas of natural law that preceded him, which saw the authority of laws deriving in some way from their moral merits. His main ideas were that the world is an organism, the universe a divine organism, and the aim of mankind is to develop toward uniting with God through the Perfect Law. This Perfect Law is dynamic and protects progress. Krause's philosophical ideas enabled people to see the law also as a dynamic, evolving set of rules.

While many assume that finger-printing is a modern invention, it can in fact be traced back to 1000 BC, when Chinese and Babylonian civilisations used fingerprints to sign legal documents. In more modern times, the Chief Administrative Officer of Bengal, William Herschel, identified workers using thumbprints in the 1880s, and in 1892 Sir Francis Galton wrote a book called, instructively, *Finger Prints*. It was a modification of these ideas by another Indian police officer, Sir Edward Henry, which formed the system adopted by Scotland Yard in 1901, and in the same year fingerprinting was used officially in the US by the New York City Civil Service Commission.

The first time fingerprinting was used as evidence in court was in June 1902 in Britain, in the case of the missing billiard balls. In a Denmark Hill house, a burglar left a dirty thumbprint on a freshly painted windowsill which the attending police officer photographed. A manual search of police fingerprint records was successful in identifying a 41-year-old labourer, Harry Jackson, who received a seven-year sentence for his theft of the billiard balls.

Fingerprinting was used very successfully at race meetings during 1903 and 1904 to identify pickpockets, but it was not until May 1905 that it was used in a murder trial. The Mask Murders on Deptford High Street were solved when a thumbprint on a cash box tray was matched to Alfred Stratton. He and his brother, Albert, were found guilty and hanged.

Three kinds of fingerprints may be found at a crime scene:
Plastic or moulded prints – are left on a soft substance. These are uncommon.
Visible prints – can be seen with the naked eye and are left when someone has something on their fingers, like a victim's blood. These are also uncommon.
Latent prints – are made by secretions of sweat or oil from a person's fingers. Invisible to the naked eye, they are revealed by, for example, dusting. This is the most common print found.

There has never been a case of two people having the same prints. Prints have ridge patterns, the number, shape and location (called minutiae) of which identify a person. Fingerprint minutiae are made up of arches, whorls and loops. About 60% of the population have loops, about 30% have whorls, but only 5% have arches. Those wishing to embark on a career on the wrong side of the law may wish to determine if they have arches, as this will automatically put them at a distinct disadvantage. However, anyone who has seen *Crime Scene Investigation* will know that whatever your fingerprint, technology is now very advanced and experts use tools like lasers and luminescence to get their match. So wear gloves.

(i)mens rea.

THE METRIC MARTYRS

Since joining the European Union in 1973, the UK has had to accept the primacy of EU law over UK legislation. It is the job of the European Court of Justice to ensure that European Law is uniformly interpreted and applied throughout the Union. Under EU law, goods must be sold in metric. In true British style, five UK market traders refused to trade in anything other than pounds and ounces as they'd always done. In 2001 the five traders lost their court battle but not before they received huge support in the UK for their noble cause of clinging to the old ways. They became known as the Metric Martyrs. The man who became their figurehead was Steve Thoburn. When police raided his stall and prosecuted him for selling bananas by the pound, he took his case through the English courts, the House of Lords, and to the European Court of Human Rights. Thoburn, of Sunderland, died in March 2004 aged 39.

BAD GUYS IN BOOKS

Famous villains from literature; they may never have gone to trial, but at least some of them were brought to justice

Big Brother, dictator from George Orwell's *1984* – got bigger.

Captain Hook, pirate from JM Barrie's *Peter Pan and Wendy* – eaten by a crocodile.

Cyclops, one-eyed monster from Homer's *The Odyssey* – blinded by Odysseus.

Dracula, vampire from Bram Stoker's *Dracula* – had his throat cut, then stabbed through heart with a bowie knife, after which he crumbled to dust.

Dr No, evil plotter from Ian Fleming's James Bond book *Dr No* – killed by James Bond.

HAL, computer from Arthur C Clarke's *2001: A Space Odyssey* – delivered comeuppance when unplugged by surviving astronaut Dave Bowman.

Jack from William Golding's *The Lord of the Flies* – became just a boy with paint on his face.

Kurtz, military officer from Joseph Conrad's *Heart of Darkness* – '... He dead.'

Mephistopheles, devil from Wolfgang von Goethe's *Faust* – continues to be evil.

Sauron, dark lord from JRR Tolkien's *Lord of the Rings* trilogy – destroyed by destruction of the One Ring.

LITERATURE AND THE LAW

A reflection on London
No city in the spacious universe
Boasts of religion more, or minds it less;
Of reformation talks and government,
Backed with an hundred Acts of Parliament,
Those useless scarecrows of neglected laws,
That miss th' effect by missing first the cause:
Thy magistrates, who should reform the town,
Punish the poor men's faults, but hide their own;
Suppress the players' booths in Smithfield Fair,
But leave the Cloisters, for their wives are there,
Where all the scenes of lewdness do appear.
Daniel Defoe, *Reformation of Manners*

Year in the eighteenth century in which Marie-Augustine Marquis de Pélier was sentenced to 50 years in prison for whistling at Queen Marie Antoinette

F is married to G. G sails to America on a boat. It is reported that the boat sinks with everyone on board drowning. F marries again six years later. Then G, alive and well, returns.

Is F guilty of bigamy?

Answer on page 153

McDONALD'S IN THE DOCK

McLibel

McDonald's is one of the most successful global fast food corporations, with restaurants in 119 countries. Its golden arches are an American icon, an image that has been stamped across the world. In 1995 it had annual income of approximately $18 billion. This doesn't mean it is universally liked, but in the past McDonald's has very successfully silenced critics through the use of libel laws – a strategy that went wrong, however, when it brought a libel prosecution against five Greenpeace activists for distributing leaflets, despite the fact that the activists hadn't written them.

Three appeared in court and apologised. The other two, Helen Steel and Dave Morris, decided to fight it out in court. The resulting case, dubbed the 'McLibel Case', became the longest trial ever in Britain, and a PR nightmare for McDonald's. With help from the international McLibel Support Campaign, Steel and Morris compiled documents to support their case which contributed to a court record of almost 60,000 pages. The trial began in 1994 and ended three years later with an 800-page judgment. Although Morris and Steel were found guilty of libel, the judge was critical of McDonald's and said that through its advertising, McDonald's did 'exploit' children, they did endanger the health of regular customers, they did have responsibility for cruelty to animals by their suppliers, and did pay their workers low wages. Steel and Morris were fined £60,000 but said they had no money, and in the light of the bad publicity already received, McDonald's didn't pursue the cash.

In January 2003, McDonald's suffered its first ever quarterly loss, the result of many factors including a fiercely competitive American fast food market. McDonald's has attempted to introduce more healthy food onto its menu, and it seems likely that the McLibel Case and its adverse publicity was a factor influencing its decision to change.

LAWYERS WHO FELL FOUL OF THE LAW

Louis Piquett was a Chicago lawyer who acted for the infamous John Dillinger, leader of the Dillinger Gang which carried out a series of armed robberies in the US in the early 1930s. Piquett himself read law but got his practising licence in 1918 as a favour from William Hale Thompson, a Republican whom Piquett helped into power with a bit of vote rigging. Piquett ran a number of scams, one of which involved the Order of St Francis. For a $10 deposit and $1 a month thereafter, 400 Franciscans paid money to Piquett which was supposed to support the Order but in fact went into his own pocket. His help for Dillinger went well beyond what was legal and included trying to help him change his fingerprints.

Following Dillinger's death, Piquett himself was arrested. In court he said: 'I am not a criminal lawyer. I am a criminal law lawyer.'

Remarkably, Piquett was acquitted on charges relating to his dealings with Dillinger. However, he was convicted on a separate charge of conspiracy, disbarred and in May 1936 began a two-year sentence. On release he worked as a bartender and never practised law again, although he did receive a pardon from Harry S Truman in 1951.

In December of that year he died of a heart attack while still trying to get his licence back.

THE LAWS OF THE MIND

Born in London in 1775, Charles Lamb studied at Christ's Hospital and was a long-time friend of the poet, Samuel Taylor Coleridge. When he was young he suffered a period of insanity from which he recovered. However, his sister also suffered mental health problems and in 1796 she murdered their mother. After a period in an asylum, she was released into his care. Charles Lamb went on to became an essayist and critic of some note. In this passage from the *Essays of Elia*, he expresses the relief of escape, not only from society's law, but perhaps also from the laws of the mind itself.

'I confess for myself that (with no great delinquencies to answer for) I am glad for a season to take an airing beyond the diocese of the strict conscience – not to live always in the precincts of the law-courts – but now and then, for a dream-while or so, to imagine a world with no meddling restrictions – to get into recesses, whither the hunter cannot follow me... I come back to my cage and my restraint the fresher and more healthy for it. I wear my shackles more contentedly for having respired the breath of an imaginary freedom.'

88 *Duration, in years, of the Penal Times, the anti-Catholic laws in force in Ireland from 1691–1779*

ASSASSINATED PRESIDENTS WORLDWIDE

Presidents who died at the hands of those taking the
law into their own hands include:

James A Garfield, US President
Shot by Charles Guiteau, 1881

Marie Francois Carnot,
President of France
*Stabbed by Cesare Giovanni
Santo Caserio, 1894*

William McKinley, US President
Shot by Leon Czolgosz, 1901

John F Kennedy, US President
*Shot by Lee Harvey
Oswald, 1963*

Wafizulah Amin,
President of Afghanistan
*Killed by KGB commandos,
1978*

Park Chung Lee,
President of South Korea
*Shot by head of Korean Central
Intelligence Agency, 1979*

Zia ur-Rahman,
President of Bangladesh
Shot by soldiers, 1981

Anwar Sadat,
President of Egypt
*Shot by Khalid Ahmed Shawki,
1981*

Muhammad Boudiaf,
Algeria's High State Council
President
*Killed while giving a
speech, 1992*

WEIRD LAWS AROUND THE WORLD

United Arab Emirates

In Abu Dhabi, United Arab Emirates (UAE) you can be arrested on the somewhat vague grounds of 'committing an action that would be harmful to the general public'. This has been interpreted to include kissing a woman on her cheek in a public place.

It is illegal to swear or make obscene gestures in public in the UAE. The penalty is a heavy fine. Likewise if you are driving a car, be sure to stay calm at all times, as even minor road rage behaviour, such as an offensive gesture, is dealt with by significant penalties. Drinking and driving is met with zero tolerance, invalidates your insurance, and also leads to severe penalties. In fact, it is an offence to drink or be drunk in public. The penalty can be imprisonment, a fine and deportation.

It is a criminal offence to eat, drink or smoke in public during Ramadan from sunrise to sunset.

Drugs are viewed very seriously, and even having a drug detected within your body is the equivalent of possession. The penalty is a minimum of four years' imprisonment.

CRIMES PUNISHABLE BY DEATH – PAST AND PRESENT

All of the following crimes have at one point been punishable by the death penalty. And as the second list shows, some still are:

1. Putting salt on a railway track.
2. Theft (first conviction).
3. Not confessing to a crime.
4. Leaving the country.
5. Train wrecking.
6. Being caught drinking coffee (second offence).
7. Capital drug trafficking.
8. Aircraft hijacking.
9. Adultery if there are four witnesses.
10. Apostacy (abandoning or renouncing one's religious faith).
11. Arson.
12. Horse theft.
13. Marrying a Jew.
14. Bigamy.
15. Theft (fifth conviction).
16. Cutting down a tree.
17. Drinking alcohol (third conviction).
18 Robbing a rabbit warren.

*Where was the death penalty applied for these crimes –
and is it still in force?*

1. In force in Alabama.
2. Britain in the 1700s.
3. Britain under Henry VIII.
4. Japan in the 1600s.
5. In force in California.
6. Turkey in the 1600s, under Sultan Murad the Third.
7. In force in Florida.
8. In force in Georgia, USA.
9. In force under Shari'ah Islamic law.
10. In force under Shari'ah Islamic law.
11. Northwest Territory in the late 1700s and early 1800s.
12. Northwest Territory in the late 1700s and early 1800s.
13. Britain under Henry VIII.
14. Northwest Territory in the late 1700s and early 1800s.
15. In force under Shari'ah Islamic law.
16. Britain in the 1700s.
17. In force under Shari'ah Islamic law.
18. *Not* in force – Britain in the 1700s.

Age when he retired in 1932 of oldest serving Supreme Court Justice, Oliver Wendell Holmes

Francis Bacon

Francis Bacon was the son of Nicolas Bacon, who was the Lord Keeper of the Seal of Elizabeth I. At the age of 12 Francis was already studying at Cambridge. He described his tutors as men of sharp wits, 'shut up in their cells of a few authors, chiefly Aristotle, their Dictator'. In 1579 he began his law career and became a barrister at Gray's Inn in 1582. He was in the House of Commons by the age of 23 and found favour with King James I. However, his law career took a dive when he was found guilty of taking a bribe while serving as a judge.

Though in disgrace, he continued throughout his life to inquire into the nature of the universe with his great intellect, and published a number of texts including *Novum Organum* in 1620, the *History of Henry VII* in 1622, and *De Augmentis Scientiarum* in 1623. However, it was one of his brilliant ideas that led to his death. While travelling through Highgate in 1626 he decided to experiment with the effects of cold on meat, bought a fowl and while filling it with snow caught a cold, which led to bronchitis, of which he died a month later.

QUOTE UNQUOTE

An unjust law is itself a species of violence.
Arrest for its breach is more so.
Mahatma Gandhi, leader of Indian nationalist movement

FISH GRASS

In Florida, the self-proclaimed fishing capital of the world, citizens can now alert the authorities to violations of fish and wildlife law online. At www.MyFWC.com you can log on and report a suspected violation of any law concerning saltwater or freshwater species or wildlife. Naturally enough, if you are dodging alligators while punting in the swamps you may have forgotten to bring your laptop or have trouble getting an internet connection. Never fear! As long as you remembered your mobile you can call the Wildlife Alert hotline on 1-888-404-FWCC (3922) – and it's a 24-hour number so even if you are fishing in the dark, you can still call. The Wildlife Conservation Commission also encourages boaters to call in suspected intoxicated boaters. If the moral satisfaction is not incentive enough, there is a reward of up to $1,000 for information leading to an arrest. The programme has been extremely successful. In 2003 approximately 3,300 arrests were made after people called in and $35,000 was paid out – an average of $10.60 reward per arrest.

SIGNIFICANT CHANGES IN
THE LAWS OF CRICKET

Although the Laws of Cricket were drawn up in the Star and Garter Pub in Pall Mall in 1774 and have remained essentially the same since, a few changes of note have been made over the years:

1809   Changes to the standard weight of a cricket ball; changes to the size of stumps and bails; and leg-before-wicket rule introduced.

1829   Size of stumps and bails changed again.

1864   Overarm bowling allowed; prior to this the ball was thrown underarm. (Australian captain Greg Chappell notoriously failed to appreciate that this Law had changed in a one-day match against New Zealand on 1 February 1981, when he asked his brother Trevor to bowl underarm so New Zealand could not hit the six they needed to draw.)

1884   Number of players set at 11. Follow-on rule brought in.

1889   Over length increased from four to five balls.

1900   Over length increased to six balls.

1922   Over length varied to eight in Australia.

1947   Over length to be either six or eight, by captains' prior agreement.

2000   Over length standardised at six balls. Umpires can give penalty runs for unfair play.

WHO IS THE QUEEN'S COUNSEL?

The position of Queen's Counsel, which becomes King's Counsel when the monarch of England is a King, came into being in 1603. Sir Francis Bacon was the first to be given the role during the reign of Elizabeth I, though he had already been granted a patent giving him preference at the Bar in 1597. The appointment was made because by the second half of the 1500s the Queen's Attorney and Queen's Solicitor were inundated with work and needed help to perform their royal legal duties. Sir Francis Bacon made the position a permanent one under King James. The services of Queen's Counsel were employed particularly in cases of importance to the State, and as representatives for the monarch they needed permission to appear in court against the Crown. This restriction on their work continued into the 1900s. The number of people appointed Queen's Counsel was very small until the twentieth century, but by the mid-1900s there were over 300 in England. Traditionally, they were barristers because the work involved was court work on behalf of the Crown. It was not until March 1997 that the first two solicitors were appointed as Queen's Counsel.

LEGAL SONGS AND CLASSICAL MUSIC

Classical music is a fitting medium for high principles. Here are a few classical pieces that contemplate things legal:

Law of the Beatitudes – Pope John Paul II
The Law of the Ladrones – Sigmund Romberg
Hear my Law, O My People – Sir David Wilkocks
The Shadow of the Law Passed Away – Slavyanka
Criminal Law – Jeremy Goldsmith
Coriolanus – Norman Law

RELIGION AND THE LAW

Christianity

Christianity is the largest religion in the world and has around one billion followers. It began 2,000 years ago and is based on the teachings of Jesus Christ, who Christians believe was both human and the son of God. Christians believe in only one God but believe that it consists of a holy trinity – Father, Son and Holy Spirit. Jesus Christ the son was sent by God the Father to earth to die for the sins of humans, thereby enabling them to reach heaven, an afterlife where humans remain for eternity in the presence of God. Those who fail to live according to God's laws are consigned to hell, where they will spend a fiery eternity away from the presence of God. Hell is presided over by Lucifer, a fallen angel cast out of heaven by God. The book of worship for Christians is the Bible, which consists of the Old and New Testaments. Islam and Judaism regard Jesus Christ as a prophet but not as the Messiah predicted in the Old Testament. Western law is based on the principles of Christianity.

IMPORTANT IMPORTING

We all know that we need to import goods, but you might be surprised at some of the laws needed to allow it to happen:

Importation of Animal Semen Order 1955
Importation of Bees Order 1978
Importation of Birds, Poultry and Hatching Eggs Order 1979
Importation of Carnation Cuttings Order 1956
Importation of Dogs and Cats Order of 1928
Importation of Horses, Asses and Mules Order 1957
Importation of Lettuce from Southern France (General Licence) Order 1953
Importation of Live Fish of the Salmon Family Order 1986
Importation of Salmonid Viscera Order 1986
Imported Food (Bivalve Molluscs and Marine Gastropods from Japan) Regulations 1992

CONSTANCE

O, lawful let it be,
That I have room with Rome to curse awhile!
Good father Cardinal, cry thou 'amen',
To my keen curses; for without my wrong,
There is no tongue hath power to curse him right.

CARDINAL PANDULPH

There's law and warrant, lady, for my curse.

CONSTANCE

And for mine too: when law can do no right,
Let it be lawful that law bar no wrong;
Law cannot give my child his kingdom here,
For he that holds his kingdom holds the law;
Therefore, since law itself is perfect wrong,
How can the law forbid my tongue to curse?

William Shakespeare, *King John, Act Three, Scene One*

INVASION OF THE BODY SNATCHERS

Body-snatching was a popular activity in Britain in the 1700s, as the advances in medical science meant there was a great demand for bodies to be dissected in medical experiments. The best place to find bodies was, of course, the graveyard, and despite its illegality and the efforts of the law to prevent it, grave robbing proliferated. Eventually, watch houses had to be built in cemeteries to guard against men with shovels who came at night to dig up fresh bodies. Even more appalling to contemplate is the fact that the well-heeled would happily pay for a dead man's teeth to replace their own, before the invention of false teeth.

Bodies are still much in demand for medical experiments. For example, in the US over 17,000 bodies are donated to science every year. Although most of these are dissected in the usual way, at least 4,000 are used in unusual experiments – bodies are used as crash test dummies, heads are used to test helmets, and arms used to test snowboard wrist braces. This use of donated bodies is seldom disclosed. Bodies are in such demand that in 2000 the police investigated willed-body (ie donated) programme personnel in a number of California universities over accusations that bodies were being sold illegally for purposes unintended by the donor. It seems that while graves may no longer be dug up at the dead of night, body snatching is still alive – if that is an appropriate term to use – and well.

STINGING NETTLES ON YOUR GROIN
– YES OR NO?

The average member of the public might be surprised to learn that violence is not necessarily unlawful. For a common assault, if no injury is caused and the person assaulted was a consenting party, it is deemed not to be an offence.

When duelling was all the rage in England, it was not considered unlawful. In 1828 it was outlawed by Lord Lansdowne's Act, but in 1837 this was modified so that it was tolerated as long as the duellers consented and there was no maiming, as maiming deprived the King of an able-bodied citizen to do his bidding.

In a similar way bare-knuckle fighting was originally allowed because it encouraged the positive qualities of fitness, skill and stamina. However, this too was outlawed in 1867 with the introduction of the Queensberry Rules, when it became obvious that it was doing more harm than good.

However, consent for acts involving injury and danger does not prevent an offence occurring. In the 1993 case of R v Brown, a group of homosexual men who belonged to a sado-masochistic club were convicted of assault causing actual bodily harm, despite the consent of those involved. Club activities included applying stinging nettles to the groin area, putting fish hooks into the penis, and more ordinary pursuits of whipping, branding and beating. The court found that it was not in the public interest to allow such dangerous activities, even if the participants are willing.

THE LAW OF ANCIENT ANGKOR

The Khmer kings ruled over a Hindu and Buddhist empire in Southeast Asia for over 500 years from 802 AD, during which time Angkor was the capital. The empire's laws were those laid down in the Code of Manu, a collection of Brahmanic laws written in the fourth century BC. Each law was etched onto stone and also onto copper, silver or gold tablets. The Khmer king was the mediator in disputes over land, while people accused of crimes appeared before magistrates called 'sabhachara'. For lesser offences fines might be levied, but the cutting off of the nose, hands or feet was also known. For a serious offence the penalty was being thrown into a ditch and having stones piled on top of you. Thieves were tortured, unless the goods alleged to be stolen could not be found. In that case, the accused person was required to thrust their hand into boiling oil. If guilty, their hand would boil away; if not it would be unharmed. Though no doubt the authorities were pleased with this system, the accused were probably not.

Amount, in millions of dollars, awarded by a New York jury against St John 95 Episcopal Hospital for improper conduct during a premature birth injury

Liquidate.

NOTORIOUS PRISONS

Devil's Island

Devil's Island was a French prison located on an island off the coast of French Guiana, although some prisoners were also kept on the mainland. The only way to escape was by boat and then on foot through dense jungle. Very few escaped and indeed few of its 80,000 plus prisoners survived at all. A book called *Dry Guillotine*, published in 1938, brought to light the appalling conditions on Devil's Island, but it was the publication of *Papillon* by an ex-convict in 1970 and the 1973 movie starring Steve McQueen that really made the prison world famous, or should we say, world infamous. Who can forget the gruelling sequence where Steve McQueen endures solitary confinement and a tasty diet of juicy looking cockroaches? Opened in 1852 by Emperor Napoleon III, the prison was closed for good in 1946. The island is now used by the European Space Agency to launch satellites, a further source of misery for the island's long-suffering cockroach population.

96 *Maximum number of hours, including extensions, that a suspect can be detained in custody*

LEGAL TEASERS

What is this an anagram for? Police catch me.
Answer on page 153

LITERATURE AND THE LAW

We spent the next six hours in a tiny concrete cell with about 20 Puerto Ricans. We couldn't sit down because they had pissed all over the floor, so we stood in the middle of the room, giving out cigarettes like representatives of the Red Cross. They were a dangerous-looking lot. Some were drunk and others seemed crazy. I felt safe as long as we could supply them with cigarettes, but I wondered what would happen when we ran out.

The guard solved this problem for us, at a nickel a cigarette. Each time we wanted one for ourselves we had to buy 20 – one for every man in the cell. After two rounds, the guard sent out for a new carton. We figured out later that our stay in the cell cost us more than 15 dollars, which Sala and I paid, since Yeamon had no money.

It seemed like we had been there for six years when the guard finally opened the door and beckoned us out.

Hunter S Thompson, *The Rum Diary*

QUOTE UNQUOTE

*So act that your principle of action might safely be
made a law for the whole world.*
Immanuel Kant, German philosopher

VIOLENT SLEEPWALKING

In a 1991 court case, a man, B, and his female friend C were watching videos at C's flat. C fell asleep. It is not known whether C chose the video or whether B took exception to her choice of movie, but while C was asleep, B attacked her with the video recorder and a bottle. Then he grabbed her around the neck. C cried out and B came to his senses and expressed remorse for his actions. When charged with wounding with intent, B argued that he was sleepwalking and didn't know what he was doing, and that he was effectively a non-insane automaton. The judge said that if he was sleepwalking then the law regards his act as one of insanity. Therefore he was not guilty. However, before B could heave a sigh of relief, the judge announced that B should be detained in a secure hospital on account of his insanity. B appealed against the judgment – and lost.

FAMOUS TV LAWYERS

Perry Mason • Ironside • Columbo
Owen Marshall, Counsellor at Law • Kavanagh QC
Rumpole of the Bailey • Matlock
Inspector Morse • Miles, Egg and
Warren (*This Life*)

WHERE UNLOADING DRUGS IS NECESSARY

In the case of Perka v The Queen in 1984, the accused mounted a successful but rather cheeky defence. The facts were as follows. The accused men were on a ship heading up the west coast of Canada toward Alaska. Rather than the standard cargo of fish, the crew were in fact transporting a hold full of marijuana. However, they began to have engine trouble and the weather took a turn for the worse. As a result they could not continue toward Alaska but were forced to head toward the Canadian coast where they ran aground. Afraid that the ship was about to sink, the Captain ordered the crew to unload their marijuana onto Canadian soil. They did so, were discovered and subsequently charged with possession of drugs. The accused argued the defence of necessity, saying that they had no choice but to unload their drugs because of the circumstances. The jury promptly acquitted them. The Crown appealed twice but the result was the same – the men were free to go. It is less clear what happened to their marijuana.

LEGAL TEASERS

Q: How many lawyers does it take to change a light bulb?
Answer on page 153

LITERATURE AND THE LAW

'Tis very plain, that considering the defectiveness of our laws, the variety of cases, the weakness of the prerogative, the power or the cunning of ill-designing men, it is possible that many great abuses may be visibly committed which cannot be legally punished: especially if we add to this that some enquiries might probably involve those whom upon other accounts it is not thought convenient to disturb. Therefore it is very false reasoning, especially in the management of public affairs, to argue that men are innocent because the law hath not pronounced them guilty.

Jonathan Swift, *The Examiner, No 39,*
The Criminals in the Late Ministry, 1711

In a 1980 UK case the facts were these: following an argument between a man and a woman, the man pushed the woman off the balcony of the flat in which they were arguing, and she fell onto the floor below. He then went downstairs, tied a rope around her neck and used it to haul her back up to the flat where he put her in a bath, cut her throat, cut up her body and got rid of it. She was never found. As it was the result of an argument, the man was charged with manslaughter rather than murder. In court, it was said that the cause of death was either:

1. The fall from the balcony; or
2. Strangulation by the rope; or
3. The cut to her throat.

As the prosecution admitted that it was impossible to prove which of these events caused death, the judge acquitted the accused on the grounds that the prosecution had failed to prove the cause of death.

However, on appeal to the Criminal Division of the Court of Appeal, Lord Justice Ackner took control of this apparently risible situation and said: 'If an accused kills another by one or other of two or more different acts each of which, if it caused the death, is a sufficient act to establish manslaughter, is it necessary, in order to found a conviction, to prove which act caused the death? The answer to that question is no, it is not necessary to found a conviction to prove which act caused the death. No authority is required to justify this answer, which is clear beyond argument.' The man was found guilty of manslaughter.

ONE FOR THE LAWYERS

A man went into a pet shop to buy a parrot. The shop owner pointed to three identical-looking parrots on a perch and said, 'The parrot on the left costs £500.'

'Why does it cost so much?' asked the customer.

The owner replied, 'Well, it knows how to do legal research.'

'OK, how much is that one?' asked the customer, pointing to the middle bird.

'One thousand pounds,' said the shop owner. 'It can do everything the other parrot can do plus it knows how to write a brief that will win any case.'

'What about that one?' asked the customer, pointing to the last parrot.

'Four thousand pounds,' said the shop owner.

'Four thousand pounds?' said the customer. 'What does it do?'

'To be honest,' said the shop owner, 'I've never seen him do a darn thing, but the other two call him Senior Partner.'

To launder money, you need to follow a three-step process:

1. Placement – you need to get your money into the global financial system.

2. Layering – you must move your money through a number of transactions and a number of 'shell' or 'brass plate' companies. These exist on paper only. Money simply passes through them, which makes it more difficult to track where it came from and where it is going. Many jurisdictions don't require corporate records to be kept, making it easy to use shell companies.

3. Integration – you must get your money back, freshly laundered, so it can be spent. There are various ways to integrate money without exposing the trail. For example, an offshore bank can issue a person with a credit or debit card, protected by confidentiality, which a person can use to spend the money; or a person may get their offshore company to 'hire' them as a 'consultant', paying generous consulting fees with maybe even a car or house thrown in for good measure; or money may be integrated in the form of a loan. The offshore company 'loans' the money to a person's local business, with the added benefit that it is non-taxable.

For integration, small Pacific Islands such as Nauru can be useful. Nauru has a population under 13,000 but in 2002 had over 400 registered banks. It is alleged that the Russian mafia were keen on Nauru, and not just for its palm trees and golden beaches. However, this anomaly drew unwanted attention to Nauru, and it was eventually blacklisted by the US government and international bodies. By early 2004, Nauru was facing bankruptcy.

At times like these a money launderer might look to bigger cities, such as Paris, Frankfurt, London, New York and Geneva, to find relative anonymity and because huge sums pass through banks in these places.

In most developed countries, transactions over a certain amount – usually around £6,000 though sometimes higher – must be reported. To avoid this, launderers use 'smurfing', a process whereby many transactions just under the limit are processed.

A more traditional way of transferring money is informal money transfer. This system, used for centuries in Southeast Asia, the Middle East and among Chinese, has two characteristics:

1. No records are involved. It relies on tokens, such as a password, and trust.

2. Money never leaves the country of origin. This method – older and often harder to crack than modern methods – is called 'hundi' in Pakistan, 'hawala' in India and 'chop' in China.

Of course, one the oldest and crudest ways to move money – filling up a suitcase and taking it across the border – is still popular. It's risky, but effective.

Dean hadn't bargained on recent cutbacks in the budget of the Witness Protection Scheme.

RELIGION AND THE LAW

Buddhism

Buddhism is a religion and philosophy based on the teachings of Siddhartha Gautama who lived between approximately 563 and 483 BC. After an early life of luxury, he became an ascetic and preached following a middle path in life which produces insight and knowledge, and leads to enlightenment and nirvana. Originating in India, Buddhism gradually spread throughout Asia to Central Asia, Tibet, Sri Lanka and Southeast Asia, as well as the East Asian countries of China, Mongolia, Korea and Japan. There are about 350 million Buddhists in the world. Buddhists do not believe in a creator God but rather in personal spiritual development. All life is connected and so there should be respect for all life, although only the Northern School of Buddhist practice forbids the eating of flesh and thus requires its followers to be vegetarian. The concepts of karma and reincarnation are central to the belief, and the ultimate aim is to reach enlightenment with the help of the Four Noble Truths:

1. To live is to suffer.
2. The source of suffering is attachment.
3. The end of suffering is possible.
4. There is a path to the end of suffering.

Number of inmates who committed suicide while detained in prisons in England and Wales in 2003 101

'What do you know about this business?' the King said to Alice.

'Nothing,' said Alice.

'Nothing WHATEVER?' persisted the King.

'Nothing whatever,' said Alice.

'That's very important,' the King said, turning to the jury. They were just beginning to write this down on their slates, when the White Rabbit interrupted: 'UNimportant, your Majesty means, of course,' he said in a very respectful tone, but frowning and making faces at him as he spoke.

'UNimportant, of course, I meant,' the King hastily said, and went on to himself in an undertone, 'important – unimportant – unimportant – important – ' as if he were trying which word sounded best.

Some of the jury wrote it down 'important,' and some 'unimportant.' Alice could see this, as she was near enough to look over their slates; 'but it doesn't matter a bit,' she thought to herself.

At this moment the King, who had been for some time busily writing in his note-book, cackled out 'Silence!' and read out from his book, 'Rule Forty-two. ALL PERSONS MORE THAN A MILE HIGH TO LEAVE THE COURT.'

Everybody looked at Alice.

'I'M not a mile high,' said Alice.

'You are,' said the King.

'Nearly two miles high,' added the Queen.

'Well, I shan't go, at any rate,' said Alice: 'besides, that's not a regular rule: you invented it just now.'

'It's the oldest rule in the book,' said the King.

'Then it ought to be Number One,' said Alice.

Lewis Carroll, *Alice in Wonderland*

HIGHEST PRISON POPULATIONS

Country	Approx number imprisoned in 2004
1. United States	2 million
2. China	1.4 million
3. Russia	920,000
4. India	280,000
5. Brazil	230,000
6. Thailand	220,000
7. Ukraine	200,000
8. South Africa	180,000
9. Iran	160,000
10. Mexico	150,000
11. Rwanda	110,000
12. Kazakhstan	80,000

102 *Age of lawyer Julia Harris, one of New York's first female immigration lawyers, on her death in 2004*

Strange Traditions

In some Amazonian tribes, eg the Chorowti, the women had a very sexy way of expressing their love for their husband – they spat in their man's face.

In ancient Britain, although the woman dressed up in a smart frock to get married, men went nude, or 'skyclad' as they were poetically fond of calling it.

In ancient Persia, a woman who died as a virgin did not miss out on the important life-step of getting married. She was married before being buried. The lucky groom was paid a fee for his services.

In Wales, there was a test before a marriage between peasants could take place. The man and the woman had to jump over a broom. If either of them failed, there could be no marriage. (*Ed: I mean, as if anyone would marry someone who couldn't manage that.*) Teutonic women of central Europe had a more challenging task, they proved their love by killing one of their husband's enemies.

In India, the Mysorian Lambadis had an unusual law regarding their marriage ceremonies – no men were allowed. The only exception was for the Brahman priest. Unfortunately for the groom, he could not attend his own marriage.

QUOTE UNQUOTE

The more laws, the less justice.
Marcus Tillius Cicero, Roman statesman and orator

A ROBE'S PROGRESS

Although the style and colour of a judge's robes are now rigidly prescribed, it was not always so. Prior to 1635, judges could wear any colour of robe that they wished, and in the medieval period they did so, perhaps to express their own unique character. However, certain elements became common, such as the lining of a robe with fine silk in the summer and animal fur in the winter, for practical reasons. This trend of conformity gradually extended to the colour of the robes themselves, which were green for the warmer seasons and bluish-purple for the cold. In the 1300s the robes were long with a short-sleeved or sleeveless jerkin over the top. By the end of that century the jerkin had been abandoned in favour of a cloak worn over the robes, which was secured on the right shoulder. Before any further permutations could occur, the dress was codified in 1635 and the robes that are worn today remain closely based on those 450-year-old rules.

A few famous pirates, some of history's least law-abiding citizens

Ariz Barbarossa, aka Red Beard A Barbary corsair active in the Mediterranean.

Richard Bishop An Englishman once elected Admiral of Atlantic pirates.

William Kidd, aka Captain Kidd His reputation was enhanced by the writings of Daniel Defoe.

Cheng I Led a large group of pirates, having been born into a pirate family.

Bart Roberts, aka Black Bart A legendary pirate who prowled the Caribbean and African coasts.

Diego Grillo, aka El Mulato Liked to rob Spanish ships.

David Herriot No relation to the kind vet, he worked ships in the Caribbean.

Sherip Shalay A Malay pirate whose favourite hunting ground was the South China Sea.

Edward Teach, aka Blackbeard Again, his reputation was helped along nicely by the writings of Daniel Defoe.

QUOTE UNQUOTE

One day is to mark the seriousness of handling a banana – that means your immediate release and that means no more bananas. Judge Esmond Faulks in Newcastle Crown Court on sentencing Paul Fletcher to one day in prison for eating a stolen banana, August 2004

LEGAL PERSONALITIES

Solon of Athens

Solon of Athens (circa 638-559 BC) was an Athenian leader who made great legal reforms. He travelled the world to make sure his laws were the best ones. According to Aristotle, Solon's most democratic reforms were these three:

1. Forbidding loans to be made on your own person, so that if you couldn't pay you wouldn't became a slave.
2. Introducing the ability of a citizen to sue another over wrongdoing. (For which lawyers are eternally grateful.)
3. Introducing the right to appeal to the dicastery, the Athenian court of justice.

It is said by Sosicrates that Solon was Archon of Athens in 594 BC, and it was during this time that he made his laws. He died at the age of 80 in Cyprus.

104 *Age of Joseph W Woodrough, who was still serving as a senior judge of the US Court of Appeals, when he died in 1977*

MUSICIANS CAUGHT GREEN-HANDED

Famous musicians arrested for possession of marijuana

Louis Armstrong – 1931
Ray Charles – 1961
Bunny Wailer – 1967
David Bowie – 1976
Neil Diamond – 1976
Iggy Pop – 1976
Carlos Santana – 1991
Willie Nelson – 1995
Notorious BIG – 1996
Queen Latifah – 1996
James Brown – 1998
Whitney Houston – 2000

POLL TAX

The Poll Tax that most people remember was the one introduced by the Conservative Government in Britain in the late 1980s. The tax was introduced first in Scotland, and in England and Wales the following year. It was the brainchild of the then Prime Minister, Margaret Thatcher, who wished to change the existing ratings system – in which tax was levied on the notional rental value of a property – to one whereby a fixed tax was levied on each adult resident. It was popularly called a poll tax because it related to individual people rather than the property in which they lived. The Poll Tax was instantly unpopular. By changing the system from the rental value of property to the number of people living in a dwelling, the tax was perceived as disadvantaging the poor at the expense of the rich. Peaceful protests turned into riots, the largest of which took place in Trafalgar Square in March 1990 when 300,000 people gathered to protest and violence broke out. In November 1990 Margaret Thatcher resigned as Prime Minister and the Poll Tax was replaced with Council Tax, which more closely resembled the old ratings system.

This was not the first time a poll tax had proven unpopular. John of Gaunt, the regent of King Richard II, levied a poll tax in 1380 to finance war against France, which led to the Peasant's Revolt of 1381. Marching on London, rebels demanded reforms to which Richard II initially agreed. However, this time the reversal was very short-lived. The day after the king agreed to reforms, he had rebel leaders killed and the rebels themselves were dispersed. The poll tax was then restored.

*Number of males, per 100,000 people, in Australia in juvenile corrective 105
institutions in 1981, compared with 44 per 100,000 in 2002*

LEGAL DRINKING

The Case is Altered pub in Five Ways, Warwickshire is a good place for a drink if you have no children, no dogs and are not hungry (it doesn't sell food). This white cottage pub has been serving drinks for 300 years. It still closes for a few hours in the middle of the day like in the good old days, and serves real ale from unusual hand pumps mounted on the casks themselves. There is an ancient billiards table and out back is a courtyard with a stone table under a chestnut tree. The pub did not, in fact, get its name from a legal case but because many years ago the landlord extended the premises into two neighbouring cottages. If you are hungry, you might want to try the Crooked House in Himley, Staffordshire. It gets its name not, in fact, from a presence of dodgy geezers running illegal scams but from the building itself. There was a mine underneath the remote pub which caused such subsidence that the structure leant 15 degrees. The building was supported, the doors rehung and floors levelled, but otherwise it is still very much a crooked house. If you want to sink a pint in the presence of an honest lawyer, you're going to have to go all the way to Monaco on the South Island of New Zealand. Overlooking the sea, the Honest Lawyer is an English-style pub with a profusion of roses growing on its facade and on the palm trees around the beach. The inside is quirky, with a tree trunk and an old boat adding to the atmosphere. It is a tradition for visiting lawyers to leave messages on beer mats and there are a great deal of these on display. Oh, and the food and drink are good.

LEGAL TEASERS

First runner out of the cross-America highway shows no will (9 letters)
Answer on page 153

FILMS FEATURING WOMEN LAWYERS

Career Woman (1936) – starring Claire Trevor
Adam's Rib (1949) – starring Katharine Hepburn
L'Amour en Fuite (1979) – starring Marie-France Pisier
The Big Easy (1987) – starring Ellen Barkin
The Accused (1988) – starring Kelly McGillis
Beaches (1988) – starring Barbara Hershey
Absolute Strangers (1991) – starring Patty Duke
A Few Good Men (1992) – starring Demi Moore
A Case for Murder (1993) – starring Jennifer Grey
Conspiracy Theory (1997) – starring Julia Roberts

FIGHT FOR THE RIGHT

In 2003, a Maori man called Rua used an unusual defence to defeat cannabis charges. In New Zealand (Aotearoa), the Tutawhenua Act 1993 guarantees Maori the right to follow their own customary laws and practices. The Act binds judges to follow it on pain of dismissal. So when Mr Rua found himself facing cannabis charges, the Tuhoe Maori Justice Authority (MJA) argued his case from the public gallery, saying that cannabis is legal under Maori customary law. The court acquitted Mr Rua, but did so on the basis that the charges were minor. When Mr Rua's brother also faced charges, the MJA went one step further and issued him a permit. It stated: 'We the full sovereign and mandated authority of Tamakaimoana/Tuhoe nations of Aotearoa do hereby give ... the authority to cultivate the herbage plant (cannabis, hemp) throughout Aotearoa. This authority empowers the holder of this document to full and exclusive rights to barter/trade throughout Aotearoa and other countries where it is legal. This authority also allows the holder to maintain the herbage plant for medicinal, personal and social uses.' A blow has been struck for the rights of indigenous peoples!

QUOTE UNQUOTE

I used to be a lawyer, but now I am a reformed character.
Woodrow Wilson, US president

FAMOUS LAWYERS

Sir Thomas Edward Scrutton

Sir Thomas Edward Scrutton (1856-1934) was one of the most influential figures in modern English commercial law. Born in London, he studied at London University where he had an outstanding academic career. Following this he went into practice, specialising in commercial law. He was a judge of the King's Bench Division from 1910 to 1916, and of the Court of Appeal from 1916 to 1934. He was renowned for his legal writing. His book, *The Contract of Affreightment as Expressed in Charter-parties and Bills of Lading*, published in 1886, is still a definitive text over 100 years later. At the end of 2004, you can still buy numerous different versions of Scrutton's *Bills of Lading*, and other works which are still important, such as his book with the rather quaint, long-winded title: *Commons and Common Fields: or, The History and Policy of the Laws Relating to Commons and Enclosures in England Being the Yorke Prize Essay of the University of Cambridge for the Year 1886*. The text may be seminal, but an award must also go to the publishers for getting that title on the spine.

Ishmael, the narrator, gives some account of the laws and regulations of the whale fishery.

Thus the most vexatious and violent disputes would often arise between the fishermen, were there not some written or unwritten, universal, undisputed law applicable to all cases.

Perhaps the only formal whaling code authorised by legislative enactment was that of Holland. It was decreed by the States-General in AD 1695. But though no other nation has ever had any written whaling law, yet the American fishermen have been their own legislators and lawyers in this matter. They have provided a system which for terse comprehensiveness surpasses Justinian's Pandects and the Bylaws of the Chinese Society for the Suppression of Meddling with other People's Business. Yes; these laws might be engraven on a Queen Anne's farthing, or the barb of a harpoon, and worn round the neck, so small are they.

I. A Fast-Fish belongs to the party fast to it.

II. A Loose-Fish is fair game for anybody who can soonest catch it.

But what plays the mischief with this masterly code is the admirable brevity of it, which necessitates a vast volume of commentaries to expound it.

Herman Melville, *Moby Dick*

TAKING THE LAW INTO THEIR OWN HANDS

Lynching is when a person accused of a crime is taken by a crowd and executed without trial. The term is associated most commonly with the lynching of blacks by whites in the United States. The lynching of Elijah Lovejoy in 1837, ironically for speaking out against lynching and slavery, was one of the earliest recorded instances of lynching in America. With the establishment of the Ku Klux Klan in 1867, following the American Civil War, lynching increased dramatically. Although it is difficult to know the exact number, as not all cases were recorded, it is likely that there were at least 5,000 cases of lynching between 1882 and 1968. Various legal attempts were made to stop the practice. However, in 1935 President Roosevelt, despite his wife being opposed to lynching, refused to support the Costigan-Wagner bill, fearing a voter backlash in the South as the bill contained provision to punish sheriffs who failed to protect their prisoners. Legal protection finally came with the Civil Rights Act 1964. However, despite this, lynching still continued in the Deep South. As recently as 1997, Henry Hayes was executed for a lynching, the first time that a white man had been executed for a crime against an African American since 1913.

Cuban cigars are prized by connoisseurs as the finest in the world, and are reputed to be rolled on the thighs of virgins. This, however, is a myth that began in the 1940s when a journalist saw women putting piles of tobacco leaves on their laps, and he indulged in a little journalistic licence. They are in fact made by workers called *torcedores* who roll them sitting at long, narrow benches.

Nevertheless, in the United States there are a lot of cigar lovers, and ever since the cigar fad of the 1990s they have been more popular than ever. The problem is that Cuba has been under a trade embargo by the US since 1962. Shortly before signing the embargo, President John F Kennedy is said to have sent his press Secretary, Pierre Salinger, to hunt around Washington for as many of Cuban's finest as he could get his hands on.

Today, US citizens must get permission to visit Cuba but are allowed to bring back up to $100-worth of goods, which includes cigars if wished, as long as they are not for resale.

Richard 'Mick' O'Connor had other ideas. In the 1990s he travelled regularly to Cuba and bought cigars which he sold for up to 800% profit in the US. However his lucrative business was brought to an end when he was caught on the Canadian border with over 1,000 cigars and convicted of conspiracy, smuggling, lying to a passport officer and trading with the enemy. He was sentenced in June 2004 to three years in federal prison, fined $60,000 and put on three years' probation. Mr O'Connor plans to appeal against his sentence, and has something of an advantage; if he can't afford the legal fees, he can always defend himself, as he is a lawyer.

IT'S THE LAW, BUT NOT AS WE KNOW IT

In the remote area of Caqueta, Colombia, many of the farmers make a living growing çoca, the basis for cocaine. Caqueta was once a lawless area, where migrant workers partied hard at night and everyone carried either a gun or a machete. The Revolutionary Armed Forces of Colombia (FARC) had put an end to that by 2000 and despite being engaged in a war with the government, the left-wing guerillas now control the region and provide law and order. Drinking is banned during the week, fighting is not allowed and anyone breaking the rules is sent to work on development projects in the forest, although punishments are not always harsh – a man accused of murder may be sentenced to as little as a year's work in the forest. FARC, however, are happy with the situation, as they take it upon themselves to tax the region's cocaine industry, taking a cut of 30%, which nets them millions of US dollars every year.

In Sweden and Denmark it's illegal to charge for a glass of water.

In Sweden it is not illegal to escape from prison.

Animal sex in Sweden is legal. It was decriminalised along with other 'sexual disorders'.

It is illegal to urinate on the street in Ireland unless you are holding the reins of a horse. In Switzerland, it is illegal for a man to urinate standing up or to flush the toilet after 10pm, if you live in an apartment.

The Australian Communications Authority (ACA) legislation forbids a modem from picking up on the first ring. If it does, your ACA modem permit is invalidated. The fine is $12,000 maximum.

In Australia, witchcraft is illegal, which includes giving a tarot or psychic reading.

In Cambodia, water guns can't be used in New Year celebrations. The only penalty is confiscation. The law was introduced when the practice of filling the guns with urine became popular.

In Morocco, if you are in a room with someone in possession of narcotics, you are liable to the same penalty even if you didn't know about it.

If you wear a skirt in Italy and you're a man, you can be arrested.

You can be fined for bathing in a public fountain in Italy. In McLough, Kansas, where the population is presumably older and less exhibitionist, it is illegal to wash your false teeth in a public drinking fountain.

It is illegal to import pork products into Yemen. The maximum penalty is death.

MURDER – HOW LOW CAN YOU GO?

According to Interpol, the countries with the lowest reported number of murders in 2000 per 100,000 population, starting with the lowest, are:

1. Iceland*
2. Senegal
3. Burkino Faso
4. Cameroon
5= Finland, Gambia, Mali, & Saudi Arabia
9. Mauritania
10. Oman

*In fact, Iceland's murder rate is so low that it is sometimes left off statistics of this kind altogether.

110 *Estimated number of witch trials, in thousands, which took place in early modern Europe*

LITERATURE AND THE LAW

In ancient times, no matter where,
A nation lived of wise men,
Who lawyers fed with special care,
Bum-bailiffs and excisemen;

Who made good laws to guard a hare,
A partridge or a pheasant,
But left the poor to nature's care:
Say, was not this right pleasant?

Who shut up men within brick walls,
Because they were indebted;
Then let them out when hunger's calls
Had them to shadows fretted;

Who paid ten thousand fools and knaves,
And twenty thousand villains,
To make their fellow-subjects slaves,
And steal their pence and shillings;

Who cut each others' throats for fun,
On land and on the water,
While half the world looked weeping on,
And half was burst with laughter.

Who to this country would not run,
Where only freedom's got at?
Where birds escape the fatal gun,
And men alone are shot at.

Anon, 1776

NOVELS FEATURING MALE LAWYERS

Death Row – William Bernhardt
The Narrows – Michael Connelly
Proof of Intent – William Coughlin
Single and Single – John LeCarre
On Cape Three Points – Christopher Wakling
The Last Best Hope – Ed McBain
The Deception – Barry Reed
Causes of Actions – John A Miller
The Associate – Phillip Margolin
Actual Innocence – Barry Siegel
Dirty Work – Stuart Woods

Suspended sentence.

QUOTE UNQUOTE

Law is the highest reason implanted in nature.
Cicero, Roman statesman and writer

LAWYERS WHO FELL FOUL OF THE LAW

Edward Froggatt was a lawyer who practised in Argyll Street near Oxford Circus in London. He came a cropper in the so-called Trial of the Detectives, in which he and about a third of the entire detective division of Scotland Yard were sentenced for their involvement with racing scams and bribes. Froggatt was sentenced in 1877 to two years' hard labour, despite an impassioned plea from the dock: 'The position in which I am placed is one of utter ruin in every way, brought about by the machinations, as your lordship must know, of these men trying to get me into their toils. If I did exceed my duty as a solicitor, I have been punished most severely and most onerously. My business has been ruined; ever since this charge has been made against me, I have been unable to do anything, and I am for the rest of my life a ruined man, because on this conviction depended my prosperity in every way.' The judge didn't buy it, and rightfully so – on his release he was immediately arrested again leaving the prison, in what was known as a gate arrest, and charged with an earlier embezzlement. He received a seven-year sentence and died in prison.

LETTERS FROM THE FRONT

Five letters home, as written by a real trainee lawyer, that prove becoming a lawyer is not all plain sailing and that it involves getting to know shady characters, not all of whom are the criminals. Names and locations have been changed to protect the newly qualified.

Dear Mum,

Day one finished. I am now officially a legal trainee. Only two years to go and I'll be a qualified lawyer. Glasgow's nicer than I expected but the office is much worse. It's in a basement, there's no natural light and every time it rains it leaks like a sieve. And it smells. A combination of smoke, cheap deodorant and criminality. My colleagues seem nice, though everything's so chaotic and frantic it's hard to know who's who and what's what. But my boss is a 'character' – early fifties, shock of grey hair, tough face and fake Armani suits complete with armpit sweat. He started calling everybody 'c***s' at the morning meeting because the 'feeing's doon'. Although it's a law firm, none of the solicitors seem to have employment contracts and they'll all be 'doon the road' if they 'dinnae stop f***ing aboot'. I just looked at the floor. Then he threatened to punch me and the other trainee in the face if he caught us 'f***ing aboot'. I hope he was joking. On the bright side I had my first very own client today. A jug-eared ginger-haired fellow, he seems like a nice guy. He told me his girlfriend had just given birth to their first child, so he'd had a few drinks and decided to 'screw a hoose' to celebrate. Caught red-handed but he seems quite cheerful about the whole thing.

Anyway, love to Dad,

H.

Dear Mum,

Six months in and you know how Dad was badgering me about 'defending people I knew were guilty'? Well I just had a young guy in accused of rape. Everyone in the office was calling him a 'dirty wee scroat' behind his back, but he said he didn't do it. In fact he seemed like a pretty nice guy. He told me how once when he was younger his mother's boyfriend, 'Uncle' T, had borrowed his hacksaw. It turned out he needed it to cut up a body. The pictures are in the office, a kind of initiation rite. There's an ankle, a knee, the bum (according to the autopsy report it contained 10ccs of semen) but no head. This Uncle T was done for murder (it wasn't his first either). Anyway, my client was eventually found not guilty by unanimous verdict at the High Court and rightly so (the alleged victim and the police were 'unreliable witnesses' apparently). He was delighted, until he found out the dole office had stopped his benefits as he'd been 'unavailable for work' during the trial. And everyone here still thinks he did it anyway.

Will be in touch,

Love,

H.

Dear Mum,

The first year of my traineeship is complete and so, on the first day of being eligible, I appeared in court. Trainees are cheap labour here, but the firm gets paid more for us to be in court than in the office so despite not knowing where to sit, when to speak or what to do, there I was. Sink or swim. Things started off OK – a deferred sentence for an ex-amateur boxer, a real bruiser. I couldn't understand a word he said, but thanks to a generous social work report and despite my irrelevant, stuttering ramblings he got a second chance. Not like the next guy. 'Don't worry,' they told me in the office, 'It won't actually call for trial today. They'll defer it again for lack of court time.' Next thing I know it's just the sheriff, the sheriff's clerk, the procurator-fiscal, me, my client, Mr D and a charge of serious assault. I desperately pretended to know what I was doing but nobody was fooled. My client was a mousy wee guy who'd never been in trouble with the law before. He was shaking even more than me, head bowed, almost weeping, mumbling how he had never hurt anybody in his life. I farted around to little effect, though the evidence seemed scant and contradictory. But it was good enough for the court. Guilty – three months in prison, the maximum available, and a bored 'Don't forget your toothbrush Mr D' from the sheriff. I was distraught. The whole thing had taken about an hour. Enraged by the injustice of it all, I felt embarrassed that I'd let my client down so badly. I even managed the old 'I'll get you out on appeal' TV routine. 'Dinnae worry, pal,' says Mr D, smirking now, 'Ah shouldnae've leathered the old c*** in the first place. Go an' gie ma dad a call an' tell him to look efter ma dug.' I couldn't believe it. Then when I got back to the office I got a proper bollocking. Not because I'd lost the case but because I hadn't maximised the feeing on it. 'Ye dinnae get paid to read the file!' Anyway, I hope all's well with you.

H.

Dear Mum,

I think I've become a true Glaswegian in the 18 months I've been here. My weight has ballooned on a diet of beer, chips and pies. The only exercise I get is driving my car, I smoke like a train and I'm even getting fond of bingo. I envy the guys I meet at the prisons with their gyms and libraries. Longer hours, obviously, but none of the paperwork. I met one the other day and we had a good chat. He's a big rugby fan and because all the other inmates like football, he was glad to have someone to speak about it with. He's doing life for murder, though. It turns out he drowned the secretary of the local chapter of the NUM in the river behind their social club with his bare hands shortly after the Miner's Strike ended. He comes from a small village and his dad had been one of the first to go back to work. A lot of bad blood seems to have spilled over after a few pints and now he's been 15 years inside. He didn't seem too bothered, though he did say as I was leaving, 'You know, son, if you had half a brain you'd be lop-sided.' So you'll be pleased to know I am officially both fat and stupid. I hope all's well.

Love,

H.

Dear Mum,

That's it. Two years done and I'm a qualified lawyer. My traineeship is at an end. I finished in style with a toilet trading trial at Airdrie District Court. It seemed appropriate, and we had some fun with the trial. The chubby, moustachioed police officers didn't look quite so pious when asked to describe the various penises involved. Flaccid or erect? Semi-erect, eh? How could you be sure? Any distinguishing features or marks? Are you sure you actually saw any of this? You weren't just imagining it? Of course both co-accused were convicted. I felt particularly sorry for the other fellow. Late fifties, ex-steelworker, grandfather, tattoos on arms and hands – he'll have some explaining to do down the pub.

Now I'm qualified I have the joys of night-time custody calls as well as the eight to six and evening prison visits routine. But at least my boss has been cleared of any financial 'irregularity' with the Legal Aid Board and the future of the firm seems secure at least in the short term. So I may still have a job at Christmas.

All my love,

H.

FAMOUS LAWYERS

Lord Mansfield

Sir William Murray, also known as Lord Mansfield (1705-93) was one of the key creators of modern law. From an aristocratic family, he was educated at Oxford and worked his way up through the political ranks to become an MP. He was also a member of cabinet, but he turned away from politics to focus on the law. As a lawyer he made a reputation for himself with an inspirational speech in the House of Commons in 1737 promoting a bill to stop Spanish assaults on merchant craft. He was made solicitor-general in 1742, attorney-general in 1754 and Chief Justice of the King's Bench in 1756. His influence was considerable on both maritime law and particularly English commercial law, of which he was the architect. In a ground-breaking judgment in 1772 he held that slavery was not recognised by English law. However, he was unpopular because of his tolerance toward Catholics. During the Gordon Riots of 1780, when Lord Gordon led an unruly protest through London to oppose proposals for Catholic emancipation, Lord Mansfield's house was burned down by rioters.

CADE

Be brave, then, for your captain is brave, and vows reformation. There shall be in England seven halfpenny loaves sold for a penny; the three-hoop'd pot shall have 10 hoops; and I will make it felony to drink small beer. All the realm shall be in common, and in Cheapside shall my pal-frey go to grass. And when I am king – as king I will be –

ALL

God save your Majesty!

CADE

I thank you, good people – there shall be no money; all shall eat and drink on my score, and I shall apparel them all in one livery, that they may agree like brothers and worship me their lord.

DICK

The first thing we do, let's kill all the lawyers.

CADE

Nay, that I mean to do. Is not this a lamentable thing, that of the skin of an innocent lamb should be made parchment? That parchment, being scribbl'd o'er, should undo a man? Some say the bee stings; but I say 'tis the bee's wax; for I did but seal once to a thing, and I was never mine own man since.

William Shakespeare, *King Henry the Sixth,*
Part Two, Act Four, Scene Two

BECOMING A JUROR

A jury is a body of persons who are sworn to consider and give a verdict on a case. Anyone on the electoral register aged between 18 and 70 may be selected to serve as a juror; even those that are not eligible are still selected at random by computer. In most instances it is only the more serious cases that require the independent opinion of a jury – typically cases of murder, rape, assault, robbery and fraud. However, in some instances juries will be required for libel cases, but this is particularly rare. Most people wonder whether or not they have to serve on the jury, and the answer is 'yes' unless they are disqualified, as it is part of our public duty. However, anyone picked can apply for a discretional discharge or even a maximum 12-month deferral. Those who do become jurors sit for an average of 10 working days, although they may have to sit for longer, depending on the case. Jurors are also paid for their loss in earnings, receiving £52.63 per week for the first 10 days; for service after that time, the juror can expect anything up to £105.28 per week.

116 *Number of solicitors, in thousands, regulated and represented in England and Wales by the Law Society*

LEGAL TERMS REDEFINED

Taking the law into his own hands.

LEGAL COCKNEY RHYMING SLANG

bank	*iron tank*
beak (magistrate)	*bubble and squeak*
copper	*grasshopper*
fake	*Sexton Blake*
fight	*read and write*
jail	*bucket and pail*
judge	*Barnaby Rudge*
liar	*holy friar*
magistrate	*garden gate*
swear	*Lord Mayor*
thief	*tea leaf*

Number of years the American Bar Association (ABA) was in existence before, 117
in 1995, a woman was made its president

DEATH PENALTY IN THE OLD TESTAMENT

The following crimes attracted the death penalty in the Old Testament:

1. Murder *(Genesis 9:6, Exodus 21:12, Numbers 35:16-21)*
2. Abuse of parents *(Exodus 21:15)*
3. Cursing parents *(Exodus 21:17)*
4. Blasphemy *(Leviticus 24:14-16, 23)*
5. Breaking the Sabbath *(Exodus 31:14, Numbers 15:32-36)*
6. Using magic *(Exodus 22:18)*
7. Fortune telling and using sorcery *(Leviticus 20:27)*
8. Bad example by religious people *(Deuteronomy 13:1-5, 18:20)*
9. Worshipping idols *(Exodus 22:20, Leviticus 20:1-5, Deuteronomy 17:2-7)*
10. To bear false testimony at a trial *(Deuteronomy 19:16, 19)*
11. Contempt of court *(Deuteronomy 17:8-13)*
12. Kidnapping *(Exodus 21:16)*

Execution could be by burning, stoning, or using a spear, sword or arrow.

QUOTE UNQUOTE

Justice is conscience, not a personal conscience but the conscience of the whole of humanity.
Alexander Solzhenitsyn, Russian novelist

THE 1,000-YEAR COURT CASE

In February 2004 a Canadian court threw out a class action lawsuit against three large tobacco companies. It had begun nine years earlier when four smokers brought the action against Tobacco Canada, Rothmans and Benson & Hedges. They argued that the tobacco companies conspired to hide the addictive nature and health risks of smoking. Up until 1972, no warnings were given by the companies about the risks of cancer and other diseases. They were seeking $1 million each.

However, the court ruled that the lawsuit did not meet the requirements of a class action. To do so, it would have to encompass everyone who'd ever smoked in Ontario. If this was the case, then the action would take approximately 1,000 years of litigation, according to Justice Warren Winkler. One can sympathise with the judge not wanting to sit on such a case, even if it would have held the dubious distinction of being the largest (not to mention longest) in Canadian history.

LEGAL TEASERS

Question: Why does the Law Society prohibit sexual
relations between a lawyer and their client?
Answer on page 153

LAWYERS WHO FELL FOUL OF THE LAW

Roy Cohn was Senator Joseph McCarthy's right-hand man during the 1950s anti-communist campaign in the US. In 1951 Cohn assisted in the prosecution of Julius and Ethel Rosenberg, who were accused of spying for the Soviets. They were both executed in Sing-Sing Prison in 1953, and though history has shown that Julius was most likely a spy, it seems that Ethel was probably not. In 1952 McCarthy appointed Cohn Chief Counsel of the Government Committee on Operations of the Senate. McCarthy claimed that there was a 'homosexual underground' that was part of the 'communist conspiracy'. In June 1950, Senate ordered an investigation into this, and many businesses sacked homosexuals for fear of being labelled communist supporters. Cohn organised the anti-homosexual propaganda campaign. However, it later emerged that he himself was a homosexual and in 1954 he officially retired.

In later years, he became well-known as a lawyer for the mob. He famously saved John Gotti, later to become New York's biggest crime boss, from a long prison sentence. While working for the Gambino crime family, Gotti was involved in a hit on James McBratney, who had killed one of Godfather Gambino's nephews. The hit was successful in that McBratney was killed; it was botched in that it was done in a bar full of witnesses and Gotti was holding the victim. Cohn, himself the son of a judge and known to have a few judges in his pocket, plea-bargained on Gotti's behalf and he served less than two years. However, Gotti was convinced that he would have beaten the charge without a plea bargain, and the 'Teflon Don' never used Cohn's services again.

In 1986 Roy Cohn was disbarred from legal practice by the State of New York for unethical and unprofessional conduct. He died of AIDS in August 1986.

TV SHOWS WITH WOMEN LAWYERS

Ally McBeal • *The Anna Nicole Show*
Homeward Bound • *Just Cause*
Legacy • *Obsessed*
Judging Amy • *West Wing*
This Life (Anna, Milly, Rachael)

I have known for many years that if you fill a court room with enough bullshit then the truth can walk in and out of the dock without ever being seen.

There are several big cases where this has been done, but it is a very dangerous game for fools to play.

Never think that the courtroom is the place where the truth is found.

Forgive me. I shouldn't gloat over such matters.

The reason most guilty men walk free is because poor old mum and dad juries simply find the evidence impossible to believe. That is why crime and the profits from crime is becoming a billion-dollar growth industry.

Simply put, Mr and Mrs average Aussie don't really believe it is all happening here. They think it is too far-fetched and only happens in America or Colombia or in the movies. Let me tell you it is happening here, madder and crazier than even I could describe.

The Australian criminal world is a totally unbelievable, bloodsoaked, insane comedy of errors. It is filled with the most unrealistic, nuttiest collection of murdering, drug-running, movie-watching Walter Mittys you will ever find.

By comparison, I think my story is quite a simple one. Some people think of things in terms of black and white, right and wrong, good and evil. But the real world is made with shades of grey. That is the world where all men have to walk, especially those in the criminal world.

Mark Brandon Read, *Chopper*

AN UNCONSCIOUS ACT

In the case of R v Sullivan (1983) 2 All ER 673, the House of Lords had to consider the situation where the appellant, 'a man of blameless character', experienced an epileptic fit and during the onset of the fit attacked an elderly man who had attempted to help him by kicking him violently around the head and body. The appellant had no recollection at all of doing this. He was charged with causing grievous bodily harm with intent and of causing grievous bodily harm.

An earlier court found that the appellant was not guilty by virtue of insanity, whereupon the appellant changed his plea to the lesser charge to guilty of assault occasioning actual bodily harm, and was sentenced to three years probation. The House of Lords did not accept the argument that the appellant had a defence because he was suffering from non-insane automatism. Despite a reluctance to label the appellant 'insane', it was obliged to do so in law and the appeal against the sentence was dismissed.

120 *Fine, in hundreds of dollars, imposed on actor Hugh Grant for lewd behaviour in 1995*

LEGALLY MARRIED

A Jewish Wedding

At a Jewish wedding, the man and woman are married under a 'hupa'. This is a square of decorated cloth supported by four poles under which the couple stand. The hupa symbolises the man's house and the fact that the woman is leaving her parents' house to live with her husband. During the ceremony, she circles him three times. One reason for this is to allow the groom time to observe the bride to make sure she is the person whom he agreed to marry. At the end of the ceremony the groom stands on and smashes a glass wrapped in cloth. The symbolism of this is two-fold: it demonstrates that the marriage is irrevocable – like a broken glass that can't be put back together, a marriage can't be reversed; and it symbolises the fragility of a relationship, and that it can be damaged or destroyed easily and must be nurtured carefully.

QUOTE UNQUOTE

The United States Government shakes a very wobbly stick at the lawbreaker, and tells him he'll go to prison if he beats the law. Lawbreakers laugh and get good lawyers. A few of the less well-to-do take the rap.

Al Capone, US gangster, in October 1931, the same month in which he was convicted of tax evasion and began an 11-year prison sentence.

FAMOUS PEOPLE WHO LEFT THE LAW

John Arlott (1914-91), British cricket commentator, was a policeman.

Arnold Bennett (1867-1931), British novelist, was a solicitor's clerk.

Geoffrey Chaucer (1340-1400), English poet, was a customs officer.

Charles Dickens (1812-70), English novelist, was a court stenographer.

Albert Einstein (1879-1955), US physicist and mathematician, was a patent office clerk.

Herman Melville (1819-91), US novelist, was a customs officer.

George Orwell (1903-50), English novelist and essayist, was a policeman.

St Matthew, Christian evangelist, was a tax collector.

Ray Reardon (1932-), snooker player, was a policeman.

Henri Rousseau (1844-1910), French painter, was a customs officer.

Billy Wilder (1906-2002), film director, was a crime reporter.

Lord Longford

Francis Aungier Pakenham (1905-2001), better known in Britain as Lord Longford, was a politician, author and reformer. After initially joining the Conservative Party, he switched to Labour and became an MP (1946-51) and a member of Cabinet (1964-68). He championed the idea of rehabilitating offenders when he presided over a number of inquiries into rehabilitation, crime and punishment, and became well-known for his campaign to release Moors Murderer Myra Hindley. Lord Longford published a number of books about crime and punishment. He also made practical contributions to penal reform, founding New Bridge in 1955, the first organisation set up to deal with the welfare of ex-prisoners. In 1963 he was chairman of the committee which recommended setting up the parole system, which is still a foundation of today's penal world. He died aged 95.

QUOTE UNQUOTE

Of the Law there can be no lesse acknowledged than that her seate is the bosome of God.
Bishop Hooker, clergyman (1604)

THE COST OF JUSTICE

The good book itself, *The Holy Bible*, has numerous entries and warnings against bribery, many of which are quite specific about the evil of a judge who accepts a bribe, rather than ruling with decent values and commonsense. 'A wicked [*man*] taketh a gift out of the bosom to pervert the ways of judgment' says the *Book of Proverbs* 17:23, King James version. However, despite these warnings the old bribe-the-judge trick is still a worrying occurrence in legal systems throughout the world.

Take, for example, a 2003 newspaper report by Kenya's *The Daily Nation*, which published a list of what it claimed it cost to bribe some judges in Kenya. The report claimed it would take 15m shillings (£105,675) to make an Appeal Judge swing in a criminal's favour. However, for the more economically challenged, a magistrate might be won over for a mere 4,000 shillings (£29). To be let off for murder, a criminal would have had to cough up a maximum of £9,856; but only a maximum of £3,536 would be needed to beat manslaughter, rape and drugs' charges. The alleged corruption in Kenya is a sobering example of the threat to justice that a corrupt legal system might pose.

122 *Number of defendants in the trial of rebels calling for independence of the Caprivi Strip in Namibia, following their uprising in 1999*

Ad hoc.

WOMEN LAWMAKERS

The countries with the most women in parliament at the beginning of 2002, as a percentage of seats in parliament, are:

1.	Sweden	45%
2.	Denmark	38%
3.	Finland	37%
4.	Netherlands	36%
5.	Norway	36.5%
6.	Cuba	36%
7.	Costa Rica	35.1%
8.	Iceland	35%
9.	Austria	34%
10.	Germany	32%

WHO WAS THE DEVIL'S ADVOCATE?

When the Roman Catholic Church began the process of canonisation, whereby a person who lived a particularly holy life was recognised as a Christian saint, the Devil's Advocate was a Canon lawyer appointed by the Church to argue against the canonisation of the proposed candidate. This was to be sure that the person was indeed fit to be a saint. In Latin, the Canon lawyer's unofficial title was *Advocatus Diaboli*, which might be better translated as the 'Devil's lawyer'. Ironically, the official title was *Fidei Defensor*, Latin for 'Defender of the Faith'.

Now the term refers to anyone who argues a position that he does not necessarily believe in, simply for the sake of arguing. Alternatively, they might do it to present a counter argument for a position in a debate to test the counter argument's validity.

This mythical advocate was the subject of a 1997 film, *The Devil's Advocate*, starring Keanu Reeves and Al Pacino. If the Devil were to come to earth as a lawyer, then it's easy enough to imagine he might be Al Pacino.

LEGAL TEASERS

This agreement can't get round the stove (8 letters)
Answer on page 153

LITERATURE AND THE LAW

New Egypt. A village somewhere in the south of England. A village nobody has ever left. Peach, the sadistic chief of police, makes sure of that.

An endless source of fascination for George, those boundaries. Marked on the map, but invisible in real life. Invisible but concrete because people had believed in them for so long. He was overawed by the power beliefs could generate. He could even hear it. Like electric fences, the boundaries seemed to hum when he approached. He knew them off by heart, as he knew the names of the twenty-nine policemen who took turns to patrol them. The twenty-nine real policemen, that is. How many dummy policemen there were he never had been able to work out. They were always moving them around.

One of Peach's inspirations, the dummy policemen. They were built out of straw, as scarecrows were, but instead of being dressed in rags they wore proper uniforms – helmets, truncheons, the lot. They stood in realistic positions throughout the village and the surrounding countryside. Their eyes always seemed to be staring at you. In poor light they looked as real as real policemen. It was an immensely cunning, uncanny and economical device.

Rupert Thomson, *Dreams of Leaving*

124 *Length in minutes of 1962 legal drama* To Kill a Mockingbird *starring Gregory Peck*

The Tulugaq Bar, also known as the 'Zoo', is in Iqaluit, a town of 5,000 people in the Canadian territory of Nunavut. Tensions between indigenous Inuit drinkers and Canadian contract workers spill over into violence on a more or less weekly basis. Laws created to control the two groups have been posted on the bars' walls. Beyond the town, a treeless permafrost stretches as far as the eye can see and as there is little to do in the town itself, being banned is a serious sanction.

One sign warns in bold letters:
The Tulugaq Bar supports a zero tolerance programme, along with a three-strikes-you're-out policy – one strike could concure [sic] from:

- *refusing to leave*
- *being too intoxicated*
- *failing to pay taxi drivers*
- *spitting on the floor*
- *loitering in the porch area*
- *threatening a staff member*
- *causing a disturbance in adjoining properties*
- *taking drinks outside*
- *continuing to ask for taxi fare*
- *taking other patrons' drinks*
- *throwing of any objects (glass, ashtrays, cans)*
- *purchasing drinks for a patron who has been cut off*

Another sign next to that one says:
Zero tolerance means barred from the premises with no chance of return! Things that would lead to this action would be:

- *drugs*
- *being removed by the Royal Canadian Mounted Police*
- *touching, grabbing any staff*
- *having three strikes against you*
- *fighting with another patron*
- *leaving children unattended*
- *bringing alcohol onto the premises*
- *fighting with any staff member*

The rules continue, and cover two whole walls. If you do get barred, the only other thing to do is rent a taxi to drive you around while you get stoned, which is a popular pastime. Or you could visit one of the illegal drinking dens in the town as bootlegging is big business. The only people, other than the Royal Canadian Mountain Police, who can apply any kind of law and order in Iqaluit are the Inuit women elders. They are held in high regard and hold regular meetings about how the town should be governed.

Number of children, in thousands, who have a father in prison in Britain in 2004 125

Fahrenheit 9/11 (2004)
Michael Moore's polemic against George 'Dubya' Bush and the invasions of Afghanistan and Iraq.

Battle of Algiers (1965)
Docu-drama about the Algerian guerilla war against the French between 1954 and 1957. Stylistically groundbreaking.

Salvador (1985)
James Woods playing Richard Boyle, a journalist heading into the dark heart of a country torn apart by conflicting ideologies – with a little outside help.

Nicaragua – No Pasaran (1984)
The Sandinistas v Somoza.

Promised Lands (1974)
Disturbing portrait of the Middle East.

Battlestar Gallactica (1978)
The Cylons are the baddies, despite the acting of the humans – Lorne Greene we're obliged to forgive; not so Richard L Hatch and Dirk Benedict.

QUOTE UNQUOTE

Necessity knows no law; I know some lawyers are the same.
Benjamin Franklin, US statesman

RELIGION AND THE LAW

Islam

Islamic law is called Shari'ah, which in Arabic means 'The path' or 'The clear, well-trodden path to water'. It is a set of rules that covers all aspects of life, both secular and religious. Though based on the Koran, it is not sourced only from this but also from traditions which themselves are based on the Hadis, the practices and sayings of Mohammed, and fatwas, the pronouncements of scholars. Indeed, Shari'ah also has roots in pre-Islamic Arabian traditions and other legal systems of the Middle East. Muslim countries enforce the Shari'ah to different extents. Iran and Saudi Arabia apply it to all areas of life, but Turkey abolished the Shari'ah in 1926 and operates a blend of Islamic and western law. This blend of legal systems is particularly evident where a Muslim country has a colonial past; for example, the laws of Muslim countries in North Africa have a strong French influence. The Shari'ah is also interpreted differently within different branches of Islam: Shi'a varies from Sunni, and within Sunni there are the Hanafi, Maliki, Shafii and Hanbali schools which vary from each other. Islam is the second most popular religion in the world after Christianity.

BOBBY ON THE BEAT

In medieval times parish officials served as policemen and were known as 'Charleys'. However, they did little to restrain crime, and corruption was rife. Later police were called 'thief-takers', the most famous of which were the Bow Street Runners. Thief-takers did not always act from noble motives. Using their knowledge of the criminal underworld, they would negotiate between criminals and victims to return stolen goods for a fee. However, some would also blackmail criminals for protection money or set people up to commit crimes, then arrest them and collect the reward money. They might also let criminals go in exchange for a share of their criminal proceeds. Nevertheless, they were the predecessors of the Day Police, the Metropolitan Police and the City Police.

The Thames Police Force, set up in 1798, was a response to the huge amount of theft from boats on the Thames. Following the success of the Royal Irish Constabulary, which Sir Robert Peel established in 1812, he was charged with a similar task in London. The Metropolitan Police was set up in 1829 and, in reference to their founder, became known as 'bobbies' or 'peelers'. They were the world's first permanent police force. Peel believed that the police should operate from a central headquarters that was also open to the public, that they should wear uniforms and be paid, and that they should patrol specific areas or 'beats' so the public would get to know them. These principles survive today and have been adopted around the world. Though police are no longer commonly referred to as bobbies or peelers, the reference to a 'bobby on the beat' remains in use.

LIFE MEANS LIFE... SOMETIMES

Far from meaning what it says, the term 'life imprisonment' varies depending which country one is in. On average life imprisonment in the UK lasts for 15 years, though the Home Secretary can give a 'whole life tariff'. In Poland it is a minimum of 25 years, while in Germany a prisoner serving a life sentence can apply for parole after 15 years. In Mexico it means a sentence between 20 and 40 years while in Greece a 'life term' is 25 years. In the United States 'life imprisonment' usually lasts until the prisoner dies. In Thailand, courts give very long sentences, particularly for drugs offences, which a prisoner is unlikely to outlive. In the UK, plans were announced in September 2004 to cut the life sentence for murder by a third, from 15 to 10 years. Lord Chief Justice Lord Woolf, Chairman of the Sentencing Guidelines Council, said that it could be reduced even further in exceptional circumstances, such as where a killer owned up to previously unsolved crimes.

Before going to sleep the previous night I had spent a long time in puzzled thought and also in carrying on inward conversations with my newly found soul. Strangely enough, I was not thinking about the baffling fact that I was enjoying the hospitality of the man I had murdered (or whom I was sure I had murdered) with my spade. I was reflecting about my name and how tantalising it was to have forgotten it. All people have names of one kind or another. Some are arbitrary labels related to the appearance of the person, some represent purely genealogical associations but most of them afford some clue as to the parents of the person named and confer a certain advantage in the execution of legal documents.

Flann O'Brien, *The Third Policeman*

QUOTE UNQUOTE

Our governments are preparing for a future without work, and that includes the petty criminals. Leisure societies lie ahead of us, like those you see on this coast. People will still work – or, rather, some people will work, but only for a decade of their lives. They will retire in their late thirties, with fifty years of idleness in front of them.

JG Ballard, novelist

WEIRD LAWS AROUND THE WORLD

Iran

The former spiritual leader of Iran, the Ayatollah Khomeini, laid down the law and made some quite specific decrees concerning sexual activity. Sexual intercourse was made illegal during fasting. To remove any doubt, he made a decree, which can be translated as 'Sex invalidates the fast, even if the vagina has been penetrated by the penis only up to the circumcision scar and if ejaculation hasn't occurred.' If penetration was not as far as the circumcision scar and there is no ejaculation, the fast was valid.

'Sperm is always impure,' the Ayatollah sagely declared. To become clean after sexual activity, you must by law carry out ablutions, the washing away of impurity. Ablution is not necessary if the sperm remains inside the woman's vagina.

A conviction for adultery can be obtained through the testimony of either four men or eight women. A woman can also convict herself by admitting to the crime three times while standing in the same spot. The death penalty can be imposed.

According to Iran's Retribution Law, the following sexual practices are illegal: fornication, pimping, prostitution and homosexual activity. The penalty for each is death.

128 *Number of arbitrators in Switzerland in 2002 – which is more than any other nation*

JUST ONE BIG JOKE

The image of lawyers has been tainted to the point that an anti-lawyer bloodlust has developed. But why is there such an unshakeable hatred for them? There are a number of theories on why we delight in deriding the 'administers of justice' so much, but it could be something to do with lawyers' fees. Hollywood also loves to portray lawyers in a nefarious light. Take the Coen Brothers' film *Intolerable Cruelty*, for instance, which virtually celebrated the average lawyer's complete lack of ethics – another reason why a person might hate them. Entire books have dedicated their pages to jokes about lawyers, and a brief internet search delivers almost two million sites with reams of anti-lawyer gags. Americans in particular seem to love to hate lawyers. But then again, America is the most litigious nation in the world, and is enthralled by real-life courtroom dramas such as the trial of OJ Simpson. But just so as not to spoil the fun, here are three of our favourite lawyer jokes:

Q: What is the problem with lawyer jokes?
A: Lawyers don't think they're funny, and no one else thinks they're jokes.

Q: What's the difference between God and an attorney?
A: God doesn't think he's an attorney.

Q: What do lawyers use for contraception?
A: Their personalities.

WATCH OUT – IT'S A FULL MOON

Popular legend has it that during a full moon people tend to become more aggressive, more suicidal, more violent and more accidents tend to happen. Thus crime statistics increase. The police and medical staff working in casualty departments have been known to note that they are busier during a full moon than at other times. The belief that the full moon causes mental disorders and strange behaviour was widespread throughout Europe in the Middle Ages (the word 'lunacy' comes from the Latin 'luna' meaning 'moon').

This strange phenomenon has been called 'the lunar effect' and, more dramatically, the 'Transylvania effect'. Beware the werewolf!

However, statistics that measure the actual incidence of crimes during lunar cycles do not support the belief – crime is evenly distributed over lunar phases, with no consistent increase when the moon is full. Seasons and weekends influence crimes, but the phase of the moon does not. So if the moon is full, don't worry – it's safe to leave the house.

HE LOVES ME...

The countries with the lowest divorce rates in 2002,
starting with the lowest, are:

1. Libya
2. Georgia
3. Mongolia
4. & 5. Armenia & Chile
6. Italy
7. Mexico
8. El Salvador
9= Macedonia and Turkey

LEGALLY MARRIED

Kerala, India

In Kerala, the Nayar and certain other tribes used to carry out a ritual marriage of their daughters when they were young girls. The practice, known as 'kettukalyanam', involved several girls in each ceremony. An adult male bridegroom, who also acted as a priest, tied a thread around the girl's neck. Then the girl's brother carried her to a decorated shed put up for the purpose at the front of the house. The bride wore a shawl, which covered her face. After the tying of the thread, the bridegroom washed his hands to sever his relationship with the girl, as the real marriage occurred after puberty. However, after the ritual marriage, there was four days of partying, culminating with a ritual bath, after which the bride returned home to continue the singing and dancing.

THE WISDOM OF SOLOMON

In the Old Testament, the wisdom of King Solomon is shown in the following story from the First Book of Kings. Two prostitutes came to see the King. They both lived in the same house and had both given birth to sons recently, one three days after the other. One woman claimed that the other woman's son died in the night because his mother lay on him. She said that this woman took her dead child and exchanged it with her healthy son. They came before the King with the surviving child and asked him to decide who was the true mother. So the King called for a sword to be brought. He ordered that the surviving child be cut in two, and half given to each woman. Then the first woman, whose son it was, cried to Solomon to not harm the child but to give it to the other woman. The second woman said, 'No, it will be neither mine nor yours – divide it.' At this, King Solomon gave the child to the first woman. 'Do not kill it,' he said, 'for this first woman is the mother.' And the people saw how wise Solomon was.

A CASE OF MISTAKEN IDENTITY

In the 1972 case of R v Collins, the judge began by describing the case thus:

'This is about as extraordinary a case as my brethren and I have ever heard either on the Bench or while at the Bar... Let me relate the facts. Were they put into a novel or portrayed on the stage, they would be regarded as being so improbable as to be unworthy of serious consideration as verging at times on farce.'

A young woman, after too much to drink, went to bed with her window open. In the middle of the night she awoke to see a figure crouched on her window sill. As the judge, by now warming to his narrative task, explained: 'The young lady then realised several things: first of all that the form in the window was that of a male; secondly that he was a naked male; and thirdly that he was a naked male with an erect penis. She also saw in the moonlight that his hair was blond. She thereupon leapt to the conclusion that her boyfriend, with whom for some time she had been on terms of regular and frequent sexual intimacy, was paying her an ardent nocturnal visit.'

She beckoned him in and it was only after sexual intercourse that she realised that it was not her boyfriend but an intruder. The man was accused of rape. However, under Section Nine of the Theft Act 1968 a person is automatically guilty of burglary also if he enters a building as a trespasser with the intention of committing rape, even if he doesn't steal anything. Did the man enter as a trespasser? The answer hinged on whether the woman invited him in, even though it was a case of false identity. 'The point is a narrow one, as narrow maybe as the window sill which is crucial to this case,' said the judge, who was by now clearly enjoying himself. The court decided that the man was not guilty.

...SHE LOVES ME NOT

The countries with the highest divorce rates in 2002, starting with the highest, are:

1. Maldives
2. Belarus
3. USA
4. Panama
5. Russia
6. Estonia
7. Puerto Rico
8. Ukraine
9. Costa Rica
10. Cuba

The highest number of recorded lynchings in the US for one year, in 1901

Judge Stromboli was occasionally criticised for his dress sense, ego and showmanship, but boy did he know how to hire a court artist.

AN AURAL ASSAULT?

Can words be an assault? For a long time, the answer to this question in England was 'No' because of the 1823 case of Meade and Belt. A group of people had gathered at a house and were singing what the court described as 'songs of menace'. Although we're not sure what a song of menace might have been in 1823, the court nevertheless stated that 'no words or singing are equivalent to an assault'.

However, it was held in the 1857 case of Light that words could constitute an assault. In that case, a man said to his wife that he'd split her head open if it weren't for the 'bloody policeman' standing outside. Then again, the court may have been influenced by the fact that at the time of the verbal assault he was also holding a sword above his wife's head.

In 1968 a court held that there was no assault when a man walked into a bank, said he had a gun, and threatened to shoot if the cashier didn't hand over all the money. This was despite the fact that he had a coat over his arm which a cashier might be forgiven for thinking covered a gun.

In modern times, courts have departed from the strict interpretation of Meade and Belt. Although it is more likely to be a verbal assault if accompanied by a threatening gesture that falls short of actual assault, such as wielding your sword at someone, the law has changed – words can be an assault.

A DANGEROUS PLACE FOR A SWIM

A walk along the West Pier in Brighton would be rather difficult today, considering its state of grand decay, not to mention illegal as it's been closed since 1975. But in the 1880s it was de rigueur to take a stroll along the said pier. One day in 1883 a man named Franklin was doing just that when he was seized by the notion that he should throw a vendor's refreshment box into the sea. The act in itself, though rash and anti-social, might not be seen as particularly grievous. Unfortunately, however, a boy was swimming beneath the pier and was killed when the box hit him. The jury found Franklin guilty of manslaughter. The case of R v Franklin (1883) 15 Cox CC 163, was an example of constructive manslaughter – constructive in that he was guilty because the death resulted from his unlawful act, albeit of lesser gravity.

Another example of this doctrine being applied was the case of Fenton (1830) 1 Lew CC 179. The defendant threw stones down a mineshaft. A stone broke some scaffolding which knocked over a wagon which killed several miners. He was found guilty of constructive manslaughter as the deaths were caused by the unlawful act of throwing the stones.

QUOTE UNQUOTE

A judge is a law student who marks his own examination papers.
HL Mencken, US journalist and literary critic

COURT IN THE ACT

Classic films about the law and lawyers

Hollywood on Trial (1976) – the House Un-American Activities Committee does its thing on Hollywood in 1947.

I Am the Law (1938) – a law professor takes on the racketeers.

I Am a Fugitive from a Chain Gang (1932) – a man is wrongly convicted of murder.

I Accuse! (1957) – Alfred Dreyfus, wrongfully imprisoned on Devil's Island in the nineteenth century, before being exonerated.

I Confess (1953) – Hitchcock movie about the sanctity of the Catholic confessional.

Juvenile Court (1973) – footage taken during one month in the juvenile court in Memphis, Tennessee.

Schiele in Prison (1980) – on Egon Schiele, an artist renowned for tortured figures with unusual genitalia. He did a lot of self-portraits. And he did time. Apparently David Bowie loved his stuff, back in the day.

Before the law stands a doorkeeper. To this doorkeeper there comes a man from the country and asks to be admitted to the law. But the doorkeeper says that he cannot at present grant him admittance. The man considers, and then asks whether that means he may be admitted later on. 'It is possible,' says the doorkeeper, 'but not at present.' Since the gate leading to the law stands open as always and the doorkeeper steps aside, the man bends down to look through the gateway into the interior. When the doorkeeper sees this he laughs and says: 'If it tempts you so, then try entering despite my prohibition. But mark: I am powerful. And I am only the lowest doorkeeper. In hall after hall stand other doorkeepers, each more powerful than the last. The mere sight of the third is more than even I can bear.' The man from the country has not expected such difficulties; the law, he thinks, should be accessible to everyone and at all times; but as he now takes a closer look at the doorkeeper in his fur coat, at his large pointed nose, his long, sparse, black Tartar beard, he decides that it is better, after all, to wait until he receives permission to enter. The doorkeeper gives him a stool and lets him sit down to one side of the door. There he sits for days and years...

'Surely everyone strives to reach the law,' says the man, 'how does it happen that for all these many years no one except me has ever asked for admittance?' The doorkeeper recognises that the man is at his end, and in order to reach his failing ears he raises his voice and bellows at him: 'No one else could ever have been admitted here, since this entrance was intended for you alone. Now I am going to close it.'

Franz Kafka,
'Before the Law', The Oxford Book of Jewish Stories

BRITAIN'S TOP 10 LAW SCHOOLS

According to *The Sunday Times*' Good University Guide 2005, Britain's top 10 law schools are:

1. Cambridge
2. Oxford
3. Durham
4. Nottingham
5. University College London
6. Edinburgh
7. London School of Economics
8. Queens, Belfast
=9. Glasgow
=9. Strathclyde

---

134 *Number of justifiable homicides by police where a cop was attacked in the US in 1982*

THE CURIOUS STATUS OF JEREMY BENTHAM

Jeremy Bentham (1748-1831) was an English philosopher, jurist and legal scholar. He was the founder of utilitarianism, which is a well-established philosophical doctrine, the essence of which is that something is right which provides the greatest good to the greatest number of people. Bentham said: 'The said truth is that it is the greatest happiness of the greatest number that is the measure of right and wrong.' A branch of the philosophy is even known as Benthamism, which says that the morality of actions is estimated and determined by their utility, and attraction to pleasure and recoil from pain are the only motives which influence human desires and actions, and that these are the sufficient explanation of ethical ideas. Although not involved in the actual creation of the University of London, Bentham is its intellectual guiding light. The founders were fond of his teachings and the university took on his idea about how education should be available to all, and it was was the first to open its doors to anyone who could afford its modest fees. A more unusual legacy of Bentham is that, in accordance with his will, his body was preserved, dressed in his clothes, and stored in a glass cabinet on his death in 1832. In 1850 it was moved to UCL. It is known as the 'Auto-Icon', and rumour has it he still attends annual meetings of the university administrators by being wheeled in, as if to symbolise his enduring presence. As the story goes, Jeremy Bentham is recorded as being present but not voting unless the motion is tied – in these situations he always votes for the proposal.

A TRAGIC CASE OF QUEUE JUMPING

In a post office in Tottenham, London in 1981, a simple act of queue-jumping set in motion a tragic chain of events. A 72-year-old man called S took exception to a 22-year-old man named M pushing in and he told him so. A fight broke out and M punched S twice, causing him to fall against C, an 89-year-old woman. S and C fell over. S suffered relatively minor injuries but C broke her thigh bone. She had an operation to replace her hip joint but despite recovering well initially, C died one week after M attacked S. The cause of death was an embolism, which was caused by the broken femur, which was caused by S falling on her, which was caused by M punching S. The court found M guilty of manslaughter, despite the fact that he had not hit C nor intended to harm her. The fact that he intended to harm one person meant that even though a different person was harmed in the process, M was still responsible.

QUOTE UNQUOTE

*Laws are spider webs through which the big flies
pass and the little ones get caught.*
Honoré de Balzac, French novelist

BARRISTERS' CHARGES

A barrister in the United Kingdom in 2004 can expect to charge the following hourly rates for their services, depending on their experience:

A barrister in the United Kingdom in 2004 can expect to earn the following annual amount for their services, depending on their experience:

1-5 years

Criminal law	£20-100	Criminal law	£20-50k
Common law	£30-100	Common law	£25-100k
Commercial law	£75-160	Commercial law	£30-125k
Tax law	£60-150	Tax law	£35-300k

5-10 years

Criminal law	£40-125	Criminal law	£30-100k
Common law	£70-180	Common law	£40-200k
Commercial law	£100-250	Commercial law	£100-300k
Tax law	£150-275	Tax law	£100-400k

Senior junior

Criminal law	£65-250	Criminal law	£60-250k
Common law	£100-250	Common law	£80-300k
Commercial law	£175-300	Commercial law	£300-600k
Tax law	£175-350	Tax law	£175-600k

Silk

Criminal law	£150-350	Criminal law	£140-500k
Common law	£150-300	Common law	£150-500k
Commercial law	£200-800	Commercial law	£350k-1.25m
Tax law	£350-1,500	Tax law	£350k-2m

All figures compiled according to the Legal 500 (UK Edition), *a legal directory of the UK's commercial law firms.*

LEGAL TEASERS

GPREMER
I was a film director with a law degree.
My first name was a palindrome. Who was I?
Answer on page 153

*Amount, in thousands of pounds, of fines and legal costs incurred in Welsh
courts by Spanish and Belgian fishing vessels in 2003 for fisheries offences*

King Henry II

King Henry II of England (1133-89) was the son of the Empress Matilda and her second husband, the Duke of Anjou. Henry, a reformer of both the law and finance, greatly improved the administration of justice and was perhaps England's greatest medieval king. He was also known as: 'Curt Mantle', because of the short cloaks he wore; 'Fitz Empress', because his mother was married to Emperor Henry V; and 'The Lion of Justice'. Henry set up courts throughout England and began the practice of allowing magistrates to decide legal cases on behalf of the Crown. During his reign the first legal textbook was written – law students may praise or curse him for this – which formed the basis of today's common law. Because of his complete reorganisation of the exchequer and his comprehensive system of judicial administration, he gained greater control over the country. His reforms were largely encapsulated in the Assizes, which gave quick and clear verdicts, issued later on in his reign, eg the Assize of Clarendon (1166), which established criminal justice procedures, courts and prisons.

GIFTS AND TAXES FROM FRANKFURT'S JEWS

As far back as 1492 there was a tradition in Frankfurt, Germany of giving jurymen 'gifts' of pepper and a spice they called 'palatin'. These gifts were called *neujahrsgeschenke an die Schoffen*. The gifts were given on New Year's day and it was the responsibility of the town's Jews to provide them. However, by 1630 it was no longer easy to obtain palatin so the Jewish Administrators announced that they would provide the next best alternative from the spice merchants – two pounds of the finest ginger. By the 1700s the gifts were of money, paid to army officials, civil servants and magistrates. In addition to having to provide the gifts, there were a variety of taxes levied solely upon the Jewish community in Frankfurt. They included:

- A night tax (*nachtgeld*) of four heller for every night an 'outside' Jew spent in the town. This tax formed part of the salaries of the town's senior and junior mayors.

- The *Opferpfennig* tax, whereby one gold guilder was payable for every Jewish person over the age of 13. This was first introduced in 1372 as a result of the town coming under the control of the German Emperor.

There was also a wealth tax, which was called Jew's tax (*Judenschatzung*), introduced in 1556. However, despite its name, this was in fact applicable to the entire population.

WEIRD LAWS AROUND THE WORLD

Canada

In Canada, a teenager cannot walk with untied shoes down the main street of Fort Qu'Appelle town.

A man may not drink with a woman in the Edmonton beer parlour in Alberta.

It is illegal to saw wood on the street in Toronto and you aren't allowed to chop wood on the footpath in Windsor, Ontario.

In Saskatoon it is against the law to catch fish with your hands. We wonder if this is to protect the fish or the fisherman.

In Windsor you can't play a musical instrument in a public park.

You can't walk around naked in your own home if you have the curtains open.

Lastly, and most importantly, anyone interrupting the vital work of the British Columbia Grasshopper Control Committee can be arrested.

QUOTE UNQUOTE

Let reverence for the laws be breathed by every American mother to the lisping babe that prattles on her lap. Let it be taught in schools, in seminaries, and in colleges. Let it be written in primers, spelling books, and in almanacs. Let it be preached from the pulpit, proclaimed in legislative halls, and enforced in the courts of justice. And, in short, let it become the political religion of the nation.
Abraham Lincoln, US President

TOP 10 UK LEGAL FIRMS

The top 10 legal firms in the United Kingdom in 2004, ranked according to the number of fee-earners employed there, are:

Name	Number of fee-earners
1. Eversheds LLP	1,836
2. DLA	1,334
3. Clifford Chance LLP	1,294
4. Allen & Overy	1,205
5. Linklaters	1,145
6. Freshfields Bruckhaus Deringer	1,135
7. Irwin Mitchell	894
8. Herbert Smith	859
9. Addleshaw Goddard	851
10. Lovells	787

LEGAL TEASERS

I inherited the freehold land of France before six (4 letters)
Answer on page 153

DISCRETIONARY LAW

The way a law-breaker is treated can vary greatly from country to country. What may be dealt with strictly in the US or Britain may invite a local solution in, for example, Mexico. Cult author William Burroughs discovered this for himself, as recounted in his book Junky. *He was waving a loaded gun around in a bar in Mexico and it seems that forfeiting the gun was considered justice enough by the local constabulary:*

'I relaxed my hold on the gun and felt it leave my hand. I half-raised my hands, palm out in a gesture of surrender.

"All right, all right," I said, and then added, "*bueno*."

The cop put away his .45. The bartender was leaning against the bar examining the gun. The man in the gray suit stood there without any expression at all.

"*Esta cargado*," – ("It's loaded") – said the bartender, without looking up from the gun.

I intended to say, "Of course – what good is an unloaded gun?" but I did not say anything. The scene was unreal and flat and pointless, as though I had forced my way into someone else's dream, the drunk wandering out onto the stage.

And I was unreal to the others, the stranger from another country. The bartender looked at me with curiosity. He gave a little shrug of puzzled disgust and slipped the gun into his waistband. There was no hate in the room. Perhaps they would have hated me if I had been closer to them.

The cop took me firmly by the arm. "*Vamonos gringo*," he said.

I walked out with the cop. I felt limp and had difficulty controlling my legs. Once I stumbled, and the cop steadied me. I was trying to convey the idea that, while I had no money on my person, I could borrow some "*de amigos*." My brain was numb. I mixed Spanish and English and the word for borrow was hidden in some filing cabinet of the mind cut off from my use by the mechanical barrier of alcohol-numbed connections. The cop shook his head. I was making an effort to reform the concept. Suddenly the cop stopped walking.

"*Andale, gringo*," he said, giving me a slight push on the shoulder. The cop stood there for a minute, watching me as I walked down the street. I waved. The cop did not respond. He turned and walked back the way he had come.

I had one peso left.'

Amount, in thousands of pounds, of the maximum compensation award for sex discrimination in 2000, according to the Employment Tribunals Service 139

Wearing the correct family tartan is of great importance to Scots and anyone of Scottish descent. Others are less concerned about the exact pattern. Indeed, originally clans wore whatever colour tartan they fancied. However in Ontario, Canada they take their tartan seriously. According to the Tartan Act 2000:

The tartan of the Province of Ontario consists of four blocks of colour.

The first block is called the mixed green block and consists of 129 threads disposed as follows:
Two white;
Twenty dark green;
Two red;
Twenty dark green;
Four red;
Two mid-green;
Two red;
Twenty-five mid-green;
Two red;
Two mid-green;
Four red;
Twenty mid-green;
Two red
Twenty dark green; and
Two white.

The second block is called the forest green block and consists of 129 threads disposed as follows:
Two white;
Twenty navy blue;
Two red;
Twenty forest green;
Four red;
Two forest green;
Two red;
Twenty-five forest green;
Two red;
Two forest green;

Four red;
Twenty forest green;
Two red;
Twenty navy blue; and
Two white.

The third block is called the mid-blue block and consists of 82 threads disposed as follows:
Two mid-blue;
Four red;
Thirty mid-blue;
Two red;
Six white;
Two red;
Thirty mid-blue;
Four red; and
Two mid-blue.

The fourth block is called the navy blue block and consists of 82 threads disposed as follows:
Two navy blue;
Four red;
Thirty navy blue;
Two red;
Six white;
Two red;
Thirty navy blue;
Four red; and
Two navy blue.

The four blocks are arranged in the following pattern so that: (a) the mixed green block is adjacent to the forest green block in the width and to the mid-blue block in the length; and (b) the forest green block is adjacent to the mixed-green block in the width and to the navy blue block in the length. Mixed green block, forest green block. Mid-blue block, navy blue block.

The pattern of the four blocks repeats across the entire width and length of the material.

As of 2004, the countries with the most number of people imprisoned per head of population were, in descending order:

1. United States
2. Russia
3. Belarus
4. Kazakhstan
5. Turkmenistan
6. Bermuda
7. Suriname
8. Bahamas
9. Ukraine
10. South Africa
11. Virgin Islands
12. Kirgizstan

LITERATURE AND THE LAW

'But what is one to do when those around one behave both wrongly and badly,' I asked.

'Behaviouristically wrongly?' he asked. 'Biochemically badly?'

'Morally wrongly and badly,' I said.

'Morals do not enter into it,' he said. 'And there is no such thing as morality – only varyingly expedient conventions. What to one race is crime, is virtue to another; crime in one era is virtue in another; even a crime in one class of society is at the same time and in the same society virtue in another class. The Dobuans in Dobu have only one moral law, and that is to hate one another: hate one another in the same way European nations used to do before the concept of nationalism became obsolete and East and West were substituted in its place. Among them, each individual is duty-bound to hate the other as West is duty-bound to hate East, among us. The only thing which saves the poor Dobuans is that they do not have such good weapons of destruction as Du Pont; nor Christianity, like the Pope.'

'Are drunk as well as sober criminals to be allowed free rein, then?' I asked.

'We live in a rather inexpedient social system,' he said. 'The Dobuans are pretty close to us. But there is one consolation, and that is that mankind can never outgrow the necessity to live in an expedient social system. It makes no difference whether people are called good or bad; we are all here; now; there is only one world in existence, and in it there prevail either expedient or inexpedient conditions for those who are alive.'

Halldor Laxness, *The Atom Station*,
translated from the Icelandic by Magnus Magnusson

Number of successful sex discrimination cases where tribunals awarded 141
compensation in 1996, which totalled £837,289

In London there are four Inns of Court – Middle Temple, Inner Temple, Gray's Inn and Lincoln's Inn. Each is an ancient, independent society where students study to be 'called to the bar', a phrase stemming from the royal summons to be a barrister. The term 'inn' derives from the accommodation where barristers and students lived in London.

Middle and Inner Temple are situated on land originally purchased by the Knights Templar, a military order founded in 1118 AD which protected Christian colonies in the Middle East following the Crusades. The name of these two Inns derived from their historical headquarters in the Dome of the Rock on the Temple Mount in Jerusalem.

Lincoln's Inn, established in the fourteenth century, probably gets its name from the Earl of Lincoln, Henry de Lacy. The site of Gray's Inn was bought by a Chief Justice, Reginald de Gray, in 1294 and law students lived there.

Each Inn is represented by a badge: the Inner Temple by a Pegasus, the Middle Temple by the 'Agnus Dei' or 'Lamb of God', Lincoln's Inn by a lion and a millrind, and the Gray's Inn by a griffin – not to be confused with the dragon that sits on a pillar in Fleet Street on what was once the Temple Bar, the boundary between the City of London and Westminster.

KANGAROO COURT

A kangaroo court is one in which little regard is paid to the rights of the accused and the trial is really for show – the result is usually already decided.

The origin of the word 'kangaroo' is in some doubt. The amusing explanation used to be that it means 'I don't know' in the language of the Australian aborigines, a mistake made by Captain Cook on asking 'What is the name of that animal?' – but this is untrue. It is possible that kangaroo, or a word phonetically similar, is the Guugu Yimidhirr word for the large black kangaroo rather than the generic term.

The origin of kangaroo court, though, comes from America rather than Australia. It is recorded being used in Texas and California during the Gold Rush, both circa 1850. The term could have referred to courts set up to settle disputes about claim-jumpers. However, at the time 'kangaroo' was a colloquial English term for anything bizarre or strange, which is the more likely reason the term came into common usage in relation to show trials in the 1850s.

142 *Amount, in millions of pounds, awarded in 2003 to two German entrepreneurs, at the time the largest jury verdict award ever to individual plaintiffs*

Coolidge's 2nd Law
*A lost article invariably shows
up after you replace it.*
Calvin Coolidge (1872-1938),
US President

Barnum's Law
*You can fool most of the people
most of the time.*
Phineas Taylor Barnum
(1810-91), American showman

Peter's Law
The unexpected always happens.
Laurence J Peter (1919-90),
Canadian writer and psychologist

Tuchman's Law
*If power corrupts, weakness in
the seat of power, with its
constant necessity of deals and
bribes and compromising
arrangements, corrupts even
more.*
Barbara W Tuchman
(1912-89), American historian

Pope's Law
*All looks yellow to a
jaundiced eye*
Alexander Pope (1688-1744),
English poet

Lec's Immutable Law
*The first requisite for
immortality is death.*
Stanislaw J Lec (1909-66),
Polish poet and satirist

AND NOTHING BUT THE TRUTH

Why are people asked to swear on the Bible in a court of law? The practice of swearing an honesty oath in court dates back to the Roman Empire. At one point it was thought that men were required to squeeze their own testicles while promising to tell the truth, the Latin for witness being 'testis'. However, it is more likely that 'testis' comes from the Greek word for 'three', the witness being a third party to look at the events of a dispute. The phrase 'the truth, the whole truth and nothing but the truth' is thought to have originated in England and had become a staple of English trials by the 13th century. Early British settlers then brought it to America. With such an array of different religions today, law courts are no longer as strict about ensuring that oaths contain a religious element. For atheists and those of non-Christian religions, the Bible can be substituted for a black book and the phrase amended. For example, a common oath in a US District Court is:

'You do affirm that all the testimony you are about to give in the case now before the court will be the truth, the whole truth, and nothing but the truth; this you do affirm under the pains and penalties of perjury.'

Despite the non-religious tenor of the statement, the phrase 'pains and penalties of perjury' retains a biblical sternness.

LEGAL TERMS REDEFINED

Heavy sentence.

QUOTE UNQUOTE

*Under the English legal system you are innocent
until you are shown to be Irish.*
Ted Whitehead, British dramatist

LITERATURE AND THE LAW

A description of London
Houses, churches, mixed together,
Streets unpleasant in all weather;
Prisons, palaces contiguous,
Gates, a bridge, the Thames irriguous.
...
Warrants, bailiffs, bills unpaid,
Lords of laundresses afraid;
Rouges that nightly rob and shoot men,
Hangmen, aldermen and footmen.

Lawyers, poets, priests, physicians,
Noble, simple, all conditions:
Worth beneath a threadbare cover,
Villainy bedaubed all over.
...
Many a beau without a shilling,
Many a widow not unwilling;
Many a bargain, if you strike it:
This is London! How d'ye like it?
John Bancks, *A Description of London*

WHAT'S YOURS IS MINE

As of 2004, the countries with the highest number of
thefts per head of population were, in descending order:
1. Sweden
2. New Zealand
3. Australia
4. United Kingdom
5. Netherlands
6. Norway
7. Belgium
8. France
9. Germany
10. United States
11. South Africa
12. Finland

THE DEATH PENALTY

As the ultimate punishment for a crime, the death penalty is still a hotly contested issue. Its murky origins as a legal punishment stretch as far back as 1800 BC when King Hammaurabi of Babylon introduced it to punish certain crimes. It has continued to be used all over the world up to the present day; in 2003 Amnesty International reported that over 1,140 people in 28 countries were executed and over 2,750 in 63 countries were sentenced to death in 2003 alone. There was a record number of executions worldwide in 2001 – over 3,040 in 31 countries. In the US in 2003, 65 people were executed in 13 states, with Texas having the highest state tally of executions (24). However, 38 states and the Federal Government have capital statutes.

Seventy-nine countries have outlawed the death penalty, the first of which was Venezuela in 1863, beating the historically liberal Netherlands by seven years. The most recent convert was Samoa in 2004. Britain abolished the death penalty for murder in 1965, but retained it for military wartime offences until 1999. Fifteen countries still permit the death penalty in exceptional circumstances, which include executions under military law and for crimes committed in wartime. Twenty-four countries allow the death penalty in law but have not used it for 10 or more years, including Algeria, Kenya, Sri Lanka and Tunisia.

The death penalty is still in use in 78 countries. For verifiable executions during 2003, the most common method was shooting. This was followed by hanging, beheading, lethal injection and, lastly, electrocution.

CITIZEN'S ARREST

In medieval times, citizen's arrests played an important part in community crime fighting. It was encouraged by the sheriffs and a citizen's power to arrest was virtually the same as a sheriff's. The right to make a citizen's arrest still exists, so if you are thinking of apprehending a wrong-doer in the near future, you might want to know where you stand.

In England and Wales, you must have reasonable grounds for believing that an offence is being committed or knowing that it has been committed. Then there are two situations in which you may make a citizen's arrest.

1. If the person you arrest is committing an arrestable offence; that is, the minimum sentence for it would be five years in prison.
2. If the person you arrest is unlawfully at large, meaning that they have escaped from prison or have broken the terms of their bail.

However, the right of citizen's arrest should be exercised with caution. If you get it wrong you could be liable to charges – and the courts have traditionally not smiled upon wrongful arrest. For example, in the 1985 case of R v Jackson, where X crashed into Y, Y attempted to prevent X leaving the scene by taking his car keys. Despite the fact that X had committed an offence, it was not an arrestable offence, so when Y was eventually dragged along the street attached to X's fleeing car, it was held to be self-defence by Y.

US citizens are also permitted to make a citizen's arrest. Again, it is necessary for them to have reasonable grounds for believing a person committed an offence before carrying out their task, although the right varies from state to state, and some even insist upon it. For example, in Kentucky you are actually required to take steps to prevent a felony occurring if you witness it. Should the would-be criminal not take kindly to being apprehended, never fear; you are permitted to kill a felon who attempts to flee while you are making a citizen's arrest. That should stop him.

MOVIE AND TV PERSONALITIES CAUGHT GREEN-HANDED

Famous movie and TV personalities arrested for possession of marijuana include:

Robert Mitchum, actor – 1948

Bob Denver (played Gilligan in *Gilligan's Island*) – 1998

Oliver Stone, filmmaker – 1999

Matthew McConaughey, actor – 1999

Brad Renfro, actor – 1999

THE LEGAL ATTITUDE TO CANNABIS

Despite being used by humans for thousands of years, it was only in the early 1900s that marijuana was outlawed in the majority of Western countries. In Britain it was made illegal in 1928 with the signing of the International Opium Convention, while in the US it was the Marijuana Tax Act 1937 that began the process of criminalisation.

Today, laws vary considerably from country to country. In Germany and Portugal, cannabis is legal for personal use. In the Netherlands, possession is a misdemeanour but a police policy of non-enforcement has meant it is effectively decriminalised – and it is available in coffee shops throughout the country. In Britain it was reclassified from Class B to Class C on 24 January 2004, meaning that police will usually not arrest people for possession or use, though it remains technically illegal.

In South Australia, Northern Territory and Australian Capital Territory, cannabis has been decriminalised providing the amount in question is small. Cannabis use is also viewed liberally in Canada and Switzerland.

QUOTE UNQUOTE

The more laws and order are made prominent,
the more thieves and robbers there will be.
Lao Tzu, Chinese Taoist Philosopher

MURPHY'S LAW

Murphy's law – that if something can go wrong, it always will – is something that seems to afflict all of us at one time or another. But who was Murphy and how did his famous pessimistic law come about? Murphy's law was named after Captain Edward A Murphy, an engineer at Edwards Air Force Base in the United States. In 1949, he and others were working on a project (MX981) to determine how much deceleration a human body can cope with. One day it transpired that an important piece of equipment had been wrongly wired up, and Captain Murphy made the comment that the technician responsible will always find a wrong way to do something if at all possible. The personnel on the base wrote a list of pithy sayings and kept them on the wall, and Murphy's was added to it. Later an Air Force doctor gave a press conference and said that their exemplary safety record was due to their awareness of Murphy's law and their desire to avoid it. The name stuck and soon aerospace manufacturers were using the saying and its reference to Murphy in advertising campaigns. Murphy's law was here to stay.

Number of US law enforcement officers that were killed in the line of 147
duty in 2002

BAKER'S DOZEN

A baker's dozen is not 12 but 13 – why is that? In the past, the selling of bread has been a serious business. During the reign of King Hammaurabi of Babylon almost 4,000 years ago, a loaf of bread and a man's hand were regarded as of equal value, or at least you could lose one for stealing the other. In medieval Britain, bread was taken very seriously from a paying customer's point of view. Bread value was determined by its weight and as bread could be sold by the dozen, baker's began to include an extra loaf in each dozen to be sure that it was at least the correct weight, as penalties for selling underweight bread were severe. A similar law applied in ancient Egypt, where it is said that a baker was liable to have his ear nailed to the door of his bakery for selling underweight bread.

There was another reason for the thirteenth loaf. During a good harvest year, more bread than could be sold locally would be baked. Bakers would then sell their dozen loaves plus one to middlemen who would take their profit from the thirteenth loaf.

THE ORIGINS OF TRIAL BY JURY

The jury system is a cornerstone of our legal system. A group of people, usually 12 in number, swear on oath to decide a verdict on factual evidence presented to them in a court. Though the institution is now widely used throughout the world, it is generally credited as being the creation of English law. However, there is considerable uncertainty as to its exact origins.

The jury system is often said to have begun during the reign of Kind Ethelred II (?968-1016 AD), or Ethelred the Unready, as he has the dubious distinction of being known. He made an ordinance that directed '12 thegns' to give evidence on oath regarding those they believed had committed a crime. Others say that it began during the time of Alfred the Great (849-99). However, its origin is also often ascribed to the Saxons or to the Normans who took the idea from the Goths. By the time the Normans conquered England in the eleventh century, they were using a form of trial by jury, although some historians claim that it was already being used in England for property (but not criminal) disputes.

The uncertainty of its origins stems partly from the fact that the practise of using a jury was never formally introduced, but instead arose slowly over a long period before and after the Norman Conquest. It was certainly being used in England in something like its current form by the time of the Grand Assize of Henry II (1133-89).

148 *Witnesses presented by the prosecution for the Kosovo indictment in the trial of the former Yugoslav President, Slobodan Milosevic*

Multiple offence.

QUOTE UNQUOTE

I don't want to know what the law is,
I want to know who the judge is.
Roy M Cohn, US lawyer

THE CONSPIRACY POLICE TAKE MATTERS
INTO THEIR OWN HANDS

Retired astronaut Buzz Aldridge found himself at the centre of a lawsuit following an incident in September 2002. One Bart Sibrel tried to bring a charge of assault against Buzz, who was one of the American astronauts to be the first to land on the moon.

A surprising number of people don't actually believe that the Americans landed a space expedition on the moon in 1969. Bart Sibrel is one of those people. Sharing some of his cartoon Simpson namesake's rebellious nature, Bart cornered Buzz and challenged him outside a Beverly Hills hotel. Bart suggested to Buzz that the moon landing was really a trick to make the Russians think they'd lost the space race. Bart tried to make Buzz swear on the Bible that he'd really been to the moon.

The result? Seventy-two-year-old Buzz took the law into his own hands and punched Bart hard in the face and walked off. When Bart later tried to bring his lawsuit against Buzz, it seemed there was no evidence that an assault ever really happened.

LAWYERS WHO FELL FOUL OF THE LAW

James Townsend Saward was a barrister with chambers at No 4, Inner Court, Temple, in London. Called to the Bar in 1840, he was a decent practitioner, but was also involved in organising robberies, receiving stolen goods and forgery, for which he earned the nickname 'Jim the Penman'. He was also involved with the Great Train Robbery, one of the great crimes of all time. In 1855, the London-Folkestone train was robbed of a consignment of gold bullion. Saward was the receiver for approximately one fifth of the haul. However, it was not because of this that he fell foul of the law. Around the same time he was discovered to be running a scam that involved duping London solicitors. Saward was sentenced to transportation for life, and it is likely that he died in Australia. Yet his name lived on, as any forger of note who made it into the press was called 'Jim the Penman'.

LEGAL TEASERS

C
DITI
AL

What type of legal discharge is this?
Answer on page 153

IGNORANCE OF YOURSELF IS NO DEFENCE

In the case of Public Prosecutions v Majewski [1976] 2 All ER 142, House of Lords, a man we shall refer to as M appealed against his conviction for assault causing actual bodily harm and assaulting a police officer. The assault happened at the Bull pub in Basildon. During the altercation M yelled at the police: 'You pigs, I'll kill you all, you fucking pigs, you bastards.' M was under the influence of drink and drugs at the time. He was appealing against his conviction on the grounds that he didn't remember anything as a result of his intoxication and therefore shouldn't be held responsible. Lord Elwyn-Jones LC framed the question of the appeal in this way: 'If a man consciously and deliberately takes alcohol and drugs not on medical prescription, but in order to escape from reality, to go "on a trip", to become hallucinated, whatever the description may be, and thereby disables himself from taking the care he might otherwise take and as a result by his subsequent actions causes injury to another – does our criminal law enable him to say that because he did not know what he was doing he lacked both intention and recklessness and accordingly is entitled to an acquittal?' The answer to that question was a unanimous no. The appeal was dismissed.

Amount in pounds required as a deposit to hire a legal wig from Ede & Ravenscroft

Committed a couple of misdemeanours, three infractions, and 27 crimes against fashion

Found 319 loopholes in 273 laws

Wondered if we might be in the wrong business on more than a few occasions

Visited four law libraries and were denied access to two

Visited police holding cells twice, voluntarily on at least one occasion

Managed to talk our way into the other two libraries, after rephrasing our grounds for entry 16 times

Began a thorough investigation into the disappearance of the last Jaffa Cake

Learned of dozens of laws we did not know existed, and thought up a dozen we felt really should

Asked 14 policemen for directions, and were told where to go on almost every occasion

Wrote seven letters to our Members of Parliament about our proposed new laws. Received no replies

Made 10 allegations against suspected Jaffa Cake hoggers, but were unable to find any conclusive evidence

Decided that laws were made to be broken

Please note that although every effort has been made to ensure accuracy in this book, the above statistics may be the result of temporarily insane minds.

Our defense is not in our armaments, nor in science, nor in going underground. Our defense is in law and order.

Albert Einstein

Number of redundancies created by the closure of law firm Dunford Ford by the Solicitors' Complaints Bureau in 1992, following serious fraud accusations

The answers. As if you needed them.

P11.   In a case in 1895 where this happened, the court initially held J was guilty, the offence being one of strict liability where knowledge by J of whether K was on or off-duty was not necessary. However, it was overturned on appeal, the judge saying it would be 'straining the law' to find J guilty where he had no intention to commit a crime and had reasonable grounds for his belief.

P20.   This situation occurred in a case and the lower courts held that B was guilty. However, on appeal to the Queen's Bench Division, it was held that B was not guilty because she did not intend T to commit the offence, despite the fact that he did.

P27.   Yes you may. What was the second question?

P35.   In this particular case, Y was found not guilty. First, as the man was not sufficiently identified nor was there a body found, there was deemed to be insufficient evidence of murder. Second, when someone is killed to protect the lives of others, it is not necessarily murder. However, if it was proved that X did drown, Y could be found guilty of murder.

P45.   No. You cannot murder someone who is already dead. However, Bob could be guilty of attempted murder. Bob believed that Bill was alive. If the facts were as he believed them, he would have committed a crime. Courts will normally hold this sufficient for a conviction for attempted murder.

P51.   No. X is not guilty of murder even if Y would not have been in the building were it not for X's actions. The chain of causation is broken by an 'act of god'.

P59.   No. Despite the fact that the wife would not have consented if she'd known her husband was infected, if was nevertheless consensual sex and there is no assault.

P70.   Fiat

P76.   The caterer

P87.   Initially, a court held F guilty in such a case in the late 1800s. However, on appeal it was held that she had no intention to commit bigamy and so should not be declared a criminal. The judge said, 'the contracting of an invalid marriage is quite misfortune enough'.

P97.   The accomplice

P98. How many can you afford?

P106. Intestate

P119. To prevent the lawyer from charging a client twice for the same service.

P124. Covenant

P136. Otto Preminger

P139. Devi

P150. Conditional

FURTHER READING

Halsbury's Laws of England, LexisNexis Butterworths Tolley

The Oxford Companion to Law, David M Walker

Legal Systems of the World, edited by Herbert M Kritzer

Criminal Law, Michael Jefferson

Butterworths Police and Criminal Evidence Act Cases, LexisNexis Butterworths Tolley

Blackstone's Police Manuals, Fraser Sampson

A Dictionary of Law, Elizabeth A. Martin

The Strange Laws of Old England, Nigel Cawthorne

EU Law, Paul Craig

English Legal System, Gary Slapper, David Kelly

Music: The business – The Essential Guide to the Law and the Deals, Ann Harrison

The World's Stupidest Laws, David Crombie

Statutes on Contract, Tort and Restitution, Francis Rose

Glanville Williams: Learning the Law, Glanville Williams

Constitutional and Administrative Law, A W Bradley, K D Ewing

European Law, Mike Cuthbert

Essential Law for Journalists, L C J McNae

Learning Legal Rules, James Holland, Julian Webb

The law isn't justice. It's a very imperfect mechanism. If you press exactly the right buttons and are also lucky, justice may show up in the answer. A mechanism is all the law was ever intended to be.

Raymond Chandler

ACKNOWLEDGEMENTS

We gratefully acknowledge permission to reprint extracts of copyright material in this book from the following authors, publishers and executors:

The Standard Edition of the Complete Psychological Works of Sigmund Freud, Vol. XXI, (1961), p 12, The Future of an Illusion. (C) 1961 The Hogarth Press and The Institute of Psycho-Analysis, London. Reproduced by arrangement with Sigmund Freud Copyrights/Paterson Marsh Ltd, London.

The Third Policeman, Flann O'Brien © 1967, by permission of HarperCollins Publishers Ltd.
The Third Policeman, Flann O'Brien reproduced by permission of AM Heath.

From *Vernon God Little* by DBC Pierre, first published in 2003 in the United States of America by Canongate Books, 841 Broadway, NewYork, NY 10003
Vernon God Little by DBC Pierre reproduced by permission of the publishers Faber and Faber Ltd

Chopper by Mark Brandon Read by kind permission of John Blake Publishing Ltd

The Rum Diary by Hunter S Thompson reproduced by permission of Bloomsbury Publishing Plc.
The Rum Diary by Hunter S Thompson reprinted with the permission of Simon and Schuster Adult Publishing Group from *The Rum Diary* by Hunter S Thompson. Copyright © 1998 by Gonzo International Corp.

Dreams of Leaving by Rupert Thomson by kind permission of Bloomsbury Publishing Plc.Copyright © 1999 Rupert Thomson. Reproduced by permission of the author c/o Rogers, Colerisge & White Ltd., 20 POwis Mews, London W11 1JN.

Extract from *Trainspotting* by Irvine Welsh published by Vinatge. Used by permission of The Random House Group Limited.

Amount, in thousands of dollars, it would cost to employ the highest paid 157
divorce lawyers in America for 11 days (261 hours) at $600 per hour

Age of Consent 50

Alcatraz 35

Alcohol 11, 14, 20, 21, 22, 63, 89, 90, 106, 125

Aldridge, Buzz 149

Allen, Woody 53

Ancient Angkor, Law of 95

Appeal 28, 47, 98, 99, 109, 150

Archer, Jeffrey 83

Aske, Robert 25

Assault 23, 59, 79,95, 116, 132, 149, 150

Avery, George 51

Babbage, Charles 52

Bacon, Francis 40, 45, 91, 92

Bagehot, Walter 77

Ballard, JG 128

Balzac, Honore de 136

Bancks, John 144

Beating of the Bounds 42

Bedlam 27

Bentham, Jeremy 135

Bierce, Ambrose 28, 45

Bismarck, Otto Von 10

Blackstone, William 59

Body-snatching 94

Buddhism 43, 62, 70, 95, 101

Canada 118, 125, 138

Cannabis, marijuana 98, 105, 107, 146, 147

Canon Law 30, 124

Capone, Al 35, 72, 121

Cardozo, Benjamin 61

Carroll, Lewis 102

Christianity 30, 47, 65, 93, 126, 141

Cicero, Marcus Tillius 103, 112

Citations 55

Citizen's Arrest 146

Cohn, Roy 119, 149

Columbine High School 31, 69

Committee of Association of American Law Schools 21

Cops 24, 33, 50, 71, 116, 139

Cowper, William 47

Cricket 92

Darwin, Charles 66

Davis, Julius Richard 72

Death Penalty 57, 90, 118, 128, 145

Defoe, Daniel 86, 104

Democracy 58

Denning, Lord 29

Descarte, Rene 49

Devil's Advocate 12, 124

Devil's Island 96, 133

Dickens, Charles 26, 36, 121

Diplomatic Immunity 16

Discretionary Law 139

Dogs 14, 20, 44, 46, 62, 93

Dominatrix Barbie 80

EU Law 85

Faulks, Judge Esmond 104

FBI 62, 68, 73

Fingerprinting 84, 88

Fish 64, 91, 93, 108

Franklin, Benjamin 126

Freud, Sigmund 29

Froggatt, Edward 112

Fulbright, J William 58

Gandhi, Mahatma 91

Gay, John 80

Grisham, John 34

Hemingway, Ernest 74

Henry II

Henry VIII 25, 47

Hinduism 61, 95

Importation 64, 93

Iran 128

Islam 126

Joan of Arc 21

Judaism 15

Judge Dredd 54

Justinian 41

Kafka, Franz 134

Kangaroo Court 142

Kant, Immanuel 97

Karma 27, 61, 101

Kennedy, Robert Francis 31
King Jr, Martin Luther 56
Krause, Karl Christian Friedrich 83
Lamb, Charles 88
Law of Averages 32
Laxness, Halldor 141
Levy, George Morton 33
Life Imprisonment 127
Lincoln, Abraham 138
Lockwood, Frank 13
Longford, Lord 122
Louis XII 48
Lynching 12, 108
Mandela, Nelson 46
Mansfield, Lord 115
Marriage 17, 38, 57, 64, 78, 121, 103, 130
Marshall, John 56
Masonic Law 22
McLibel 87
Melville, Herman 108, 121
Mencken, HL 133
Milton, John 26
Money Laundering 100
Moore, Michael 31, 126
Morrison, Jim 81
Mortimer, John 80
Murphy's Law 58, 147
Music 36, 39, 58, 66, 68, 69, 93, 105, 138
Nixon, Richard 67
Nuremberg Trials 19
O'Brien, Flann 128
Old Bailey, the 13
Orwell, George 86, 121
Phillips, Kenneth 20
Pierre, DBC 11
'Pig' 41, 150
Piquett, Louis 88
Pirates 104
Plato 82
Poe, Edgar Allan 82
Poker 71
Pope, Alexander 70, 143
Poll Tax 105

Queen's Counsel 92
Read, Mark Brandon 120
Reagan, Ronald 78
Reasonable Doubt 11
Robben Island 46
Robbery 10, 40, 62, 88, 90, 94, 116, 144
Samurai, Way of the 43
Saward, James Townsend 150
Scrutton, Sir Thomas Edward 107
Serial Killers 16, 62
Shakespeare, William 94, 116
Shaw, George Bernard 70
Shelly, Mary 75
Shinto 70
Sikhism 27
Singapore 24, 81
Solon of Athens 104
Solzhenitsyn, Alexander 118
Spandau Prison 19
Sparrow, Gerald 18
Speeding Ticket 33
Stoker, Bram 23, 86
Swift, Jonathan 60, 98
Tartan 140
Thailand 18, 48, 62, 102, 127
Theft 40, 62, 77, 84, 90, 145
Thompson, Hunter S 97
Thomson, Rupert 124
Tocqueville, Alexis de 34
Tulugaq Bar 125
Turpin, Dick 59
Twain, Mark 25
Tzu, Lao 147
United Arab Emirates 89
Vaughan, Sir John 74
Verges, Jacques 12
Wallace, William 18, 53
Wells, HG 18
Welsh, Irvine 15
Westminster Hall 53
Whitehead, Ted 144
Wig, Judge's 10, 17, 37
Wilde, Oscar 13, 55
Wilson, Woodrow 107
Witchcraft 21, 110

FILL YOUR BOOKSHELF AND YOUR MIND

The Birdwatcher's Companion Twitchers, birders, ornithologists and garden-tickers: there are many species of birdwatcher, and you're all catered for by this unique book. ISBN 1-86105-833-0

The Cook's Companion Whether your taste is for foie gras or fry-ups, this tasty compilation is an essential ingredient in any kitchen, boiling over with foodie fact and fiction. ISBN 1-86105-772-5

The Gardener's Companion For anyone who has ever put on a pair of gloves, picked up a spade and gone out into the garden in search of flowers, beauty and inspiration. ISBN 1-86105-771-7

The Golfer's Companion Bogeys and shanking, plus fours and six irons, the alleged etiquette of caddies – all you need to know about the heaven and hell of golf is in this unique book. ISBN 1-86105-834-9

The Ideas Companion This fascinating book tells the stories behind the trademarks, inventions, and brands that we come across every day. ISBN 1-86105-835-7

The Legal Companion From lawmakers to lawbreakers, this fascinating compilation offers a view of the oddities, quirks, origins and stories behind the legal world. ISBN 1-86105-838-1

The Literary Companion Whether your Dickens is Charles or Monica, your Stein Gertrude or Franken, here's your book. Literary fact and fiction from Rebecca East to Vita Sackville-West. ISBN 1-86105-798-9

The London Companion From Edgware to Morden, Upminster to Ealing, here's your chance to explore the history and mystery of the most exciting capital city in the world. ISBN 1-86105-799-7

The Moviegoer's Companion Explore the strange and wonderful world of movies, actors, cinemas and salty popcorn in all their glamorous glory from film noir to Matt LeBlanc. ISBN 1-86105-797-0

The Politics Companion The history, myths, great leaders and greater liars of international politics are all gathered around the hustings in this remarkable compilation. ISBN 1-86105-796-2

The Sailing Companion This is the book for everyone who knows their starboard from their stinkpot, and their Raggie from their stern – and anybody who wants to find out. ISBN 1-86105-839-X

The Traveller's Companion For anyone who's ever stared at a distant plane, wondered where it's going, and spent the rest of the day dreaming of faraway lands. ISBN 1-86105-773-3

The Walker's Companion If you've ever laced a sturdy boot, packed a cheese sandwich, and stepped out in search of stimulation and contemplation, then this book is for you. ISBN 1-86105-825-X

The Wildlife Companion Animal amazements, ornithological oddities and botanical beauties abound in this compilation of natural need-to-knows and nonsense for wildlife-lovers. ISBN 1-86105-770-9